THE LITERATURE

OF THE

SECOND CENTURY.

THE LITERATURE

OF THE

SECOND CENTURY.

Short Studies in Christian Evidences.

BY

F. R. WYNNE, D.D. J. H. BERNARD, B.D.
AND S. HEMPHILL, B.D.

London:

HODDER AND STOUGHTON,

27, PATERNOSTER ROW.

MDCCCXCI

BUTLER & TANNER,
THE SELWOOD PRINTING WORKS,
FROME, AND LONDON.

PREFATORY NOTE.

THE lectures printed in this volume were read to a popular audience at the Alexandra College, Dublin, in the spring of 1890, and were not originally written for publication. They do not pretend to originality, nor do they profess to give a complete account of the subjects with which they deal ; but pains have been taken to insure accuracy as to statements of fact. They are now published at the request of the Christian Evidence Committee of the Y.W.C.A., under whose auspices they were delivered, and in the hope that they may be useful to some who, without the opportunity of consulting formal treatises, are yet interested in problems which bear upon the reasonableness of the Christian hope.

CONTENTS.

vii

CONTENTS.

LECTURE V.

LECTURE VI.

By Rev. Samuel Hemphill, B.D.,
Rector of Westport, Professor of Biblical Greek
in the University of Dublin.

LECTURE I.

THE EVIDENCE TO CHRISTIANITY SUPPLIED BY THE LITERATURE OF THE SUB-APOSTOLIC AGE.

BY REV. CANON WYNNE, D.D.

NOTICE TO LECTURES I. AND II.

THE information given in these Lectures as to the dates, authorship, and genuineness of the relics of Christian antiquity referred to, has been chiefly gathered from the following authorities :

BISHOP LIGHTFOOT'S *Apostolic Fathers.*
BISHOP WESTCOTT'S *Canon of the New Testament.*
SANDAY'S *Gospels in the Second Century.*
SMITH'S *Dictionary of Christian Biography :* Article " Apostolic Fathers."
SALMON'S *Introduction to the New Testament.*

The extracts from early writers have been taken partly from Bishop Lightfoot's translation, and partly from the *Ancient and Modern Library of Theological Literature* (GRIFFITH, FARRAN & Co.).

LECTURE I.

WHEN we look into the starry sky
at a certain season of the year, we
see a splendid planet called Jupiter. We
cannot help being delighted with its glory
and beauty. If we examine this planet carefully through a telescope, we shall find that
there revolve around it several other shining
bodies or moons. They are so small that to
the naked eye their light is merged in that of
the great planet. But in reality some light
is transmitted to us by them which would
otherwise have been lost, and by their move-
ments and their relations with one another
and with the central body important knowledge is conveyed to us.

As we look back through the ages of the
past, we see plainly one splendid moral
phenomenon. It is the picture of the Lord
Jesus and the story of the Lord Jesus given
to us in the gospels. This is the clearest and
strongest evidence for Christianity. The best
proof you can have of the planet's shining
is to look at its light. The most convincing
proof of the reality of Christ's existence, of
the divinity of His nature, of the truth of
His teaching, is to read the story of what
He did and said. When other evidence has
failed, many have been persuaded by this
alone. They have found an irresistible re-
sponse in their moral nature to the gospel
ideal of goodness. They have felt that the
simple and artless story of facts in the
history of Jesus could not possibly have been
either purposely fabricated or gradually
evolved. There is what is called an instinctive perception of the difference between
truth and fiction, which is doubtless the
result of long experience gained almost
unconsciously amidst the continual judg-

ments of daily life; and this perception has made the account of Christ's sublime works and noble words bear with it an incontestable witness to its own truth.

Nevertheless it is very important to be able to supplement such instinctive judgment by definite knowledge. It is well to have clear information which makes us sure that the accounts we have of our Saviour's life are the genuine products of the age in which He lived, that the story we feel to be so beautiful is really the story told by His own companions, and that the words that thrill in our consciences to-day and the exhibitions of Divine Power before which our spirits bow in reverence have come to us directly from eye-witnesses to His majesty.

In this we are helped by the documents which I have now to describe. They are, like the satellites of the planet, almost lost in its glory. They are, in comparison to the apostolic writings, poor and insignificant; yet they give us information which enables us to appreciate more exactly the

value of those writings. Their little glimmer
helps us to weigh and measure the orb in
whose light they are effaced. I wish to bring
before you in this paper the testimony to the
truth of Christianity which is borne by the
literature of the sub-apostolic age. The "apostolic age" is the time during which apostles
of the Lord Jesus lived ; the "sub-apostolic"
is the time immediately succeeding, during
which men lived who were born before all the
apostles had died. The period is not defined
by any precise limits ; but supposing some of
the apostles to have been a few years younger
than our Lord, they may be supposed to have
lived to A.D. 80 or 90. There is a very
ancient tradition that St. John died at a very
advanced age, about A.D. 100. The generation after the apostles could hardly have been
extinct till the middle of the second century.
In this paper, however, I use the term sub-
apostolic as embracing the close of the first
century and the earlier part of the second, or,
approximately speaking, from A.D. 80 to 120.
Three writers of these years are called

"*apostolic Fathers*," because there is reason to believe that in their youth they came under the direct personal influence of some of the apostles. Their names are Clement, Ignatius, and Polycarp. The other writings that come down to us from that period are few in number, and all are very poor in comparison to the grand literature that emanates from the apostolic age. While the men lived who had been companions and pupils of the Lord Jesus, and who had been commissioned by Him to teach in His name, while the remembrance of His glorious presence was fresh, and the echoes of His own words ringing clearly in their hearts, a great number of beautiful writings were sent out into the world, either composed by themselves, or containing the substance of their well-known instructions. After the apostles died, although the Church spread with marvellous rapidity, yet the number of those who taught it by writing does not seem to have kept pace with its increase. The minds of Christians still looked back to the apostles; and their "memoirs" (as Justin Martyr calls them), their "traditions," the truths they had handed down from their Master, were the staple food of the Church's life. And means of spreading literature in those days, we must remember, were tedious and insecure. There were no printers, no publishers, no reviewers. Slowly and with difficulty from one city to another, carried by stray travellers in unwieldy parchment rolls, the written thoughts had to make their way. Those that have survived in the hard struggle for existence are probably few in comparison to those that have perished. Particularly hard the struggle must have been in the early Christian Church, whose members had to hold their faith in spite of popular prejudice and religious jealousies, ready to break out at any moment into fierce persecution. Thus the sub-apostolic writings which we read to-day are like the fossils found in much disturbed strata, a few scattered remnants of a fauna and flora most of which has perished; specimens which are precious as showing, not the quantity, but the kind of organisms that characterized the period to which they belonged.

The principal writings which have come down to us from the close of the first and the beginning of the second century are the following :

1. A letter called *The Epistle of Clement to the Corinthians.*

2. A letter or address called *The Epistle of Barnabas.*

3. Seven letters by Ignatius, Bishop of Antioch.

4. A letter by Polycarp, Bishop of Smyrna.

5. A curious and somewhat visionary book called *The Shepherd of Hermas.*

There is also an interesting document, lately discovered, called *The Teaching of the Twelve Apostles*, which is generally ranked as belonging to the sub-apostolic age. The treatise, after careful analysis, has been shown to consist of two elements—one Jewish, which is probably older than the

Christian era ; the other added by perhaps more than one Christian hand during the period we are considering. As, however, there are many literary difficulties in fixing the date of its issue in its present form, and as I wish to direct your attention only to evidence as to which we can be quite sure, I shall not include the *Didache* in this study. I purpose to give you some brief information about the other documents I have named, to quote some characteristic extracts from each of them, and then to show you the nature of the testimony they bear to the truth of Christianity.

But before doing this, I must ask your attention to two other well-known documents which belong to the same age. They are written, not by believers in Christianity, but by heathens. (1) The historian Tacitus has a brief allusion to the Christian religion in his *Annals*. Tacitus was "prætor" of Rome under the emperor Domitian, A.D. 88, and consul under Nerva, A.D. 97. He wrote his *Annals* in the beginning of the second

century.   After describing the terrible fire
which took place in Rome, in the tenth year
of Nero's reign, A.D. 64, which Nero himself
was suspected of having caused, Tacitus
goes on to say :

" To   suppress   therefore   this   common
rumour, Nero procured others to be accused,
and   inflicted   exquisite   punishment   upon
those people, who were in abhorrence for
their crimes, and were commonly known by
the name of Christians.

" They   had   their   denomination   from
Christus, who in the reign of Tiberius was
put to death as a criminal by the procurator
Pontius Pilate.   This pernicious superstition,
though checked for a while, broke out again,
and spread, not only over Judea, the source
of this evil, but   reached   the   city   also ;
whither flow from all quarters all things vile
and shameful, and where they find shelter
and encouragement.

" At first they only were apprehended who
confessed themselves of that sect ; afterwards
a vast multitude, discovered by them : all

which were condemned, not so much for the crime of burning the city, as for their enmity to mankind. Their executions were so contrived as to expose them to derision and contempt. Some were covered over with the skins of wild beasts, and torn to pieces by dogs ; some were crucified ; others, having been daubed over with combustible materials, were set up as lights in the night time, and thus burned to death.

" Nero made use of his own gardens as a theatre upon this occasion, and also exhibited the diversions of the circus, sometimes standing in the crowds as a spectator, in the habit of a charioteer, at other times driving a chariot himself ; till at length these men, though really criminal and deserving exemplary punishment, began to be commiserated, as people who were destroyed, not out of regard to the public welfare, but only to gratify the cruelty of one man."

The second document is the letter of the younger Pliny to the emperor Trajan, written about A.D. 112. Trajan died in A.D. 117.

The genuineness of this letter, as well as of the passage in the *Annals* of Tacitus, has passed through the crucible of the most searching modern criticism. The letter runs as follows:

"It is my constant custom, sir, to refer myself to you in all matters concerning which I have any doubt. For who can better direct me where I hesitate, or instruct me where I am ignorant? I have never been present at any trials of Christians; so that I know not well what is the subject-matter of punishment, or of inquiry, or what strictness ought to be used in either. Nor have I been a little perplexed to determine whether any difference ought to be made upon account of age, or whether the young and tender, and the full-grown and robust, ought to be treated all alike; whether repentance should entitle to pardon, or whether all who have once been Christians ought to be punished, though they are now no longer so; whether the name itself, although no crimes be detected, or crimes only belonging to the name ought to be punished. Concerning all these things I am in doubt. In the meantime I have taken this course with all who have been brought before me and have been accused as Christians.

" I have put the question to them whether they were Christians. Upon their confessing to me that they were, I repeated the question a second and a third time, threatening also to punish them with death. Such as still persisted, I ordered away to be punished ; for it was no doubt with me, whatever might be the nature of their opinion, that contumacy and inflexible obstinacy ought to be punished. There were others of the same infatuation, whom, because they are Roman citizens, I have noted down to be sent to the city.

" In a short time the crime spreading itself, even whilst under persecution, as is usual in such cases, divers sorts of people came in my way. An information was presented to me without mentioning the author, containing the names of many persons, who upon examination denied that they were Christians, or had ever been so ; who repeated after me an invocation of the gods, and with wine and frankincense made supplication to your image, which for that purpose I have caused to be brought and set before them, together with the statues of the deities. Moreover, they reviled the name of Christ. None of which things, as is said, they who are really Christians can by any means be compelled to do. These, therefore, I thought proper to discharge.

" Others were named by an informer, who at first confessed themselves Christians, and afterwards denied it. The rest said they had been Christians, but had left them ; some three years ago, some longer, and one, or more, above twenty years.

" They all worshipped your image, and the statues of the gods ; these also reviled Christ. They affirmed that the whole of their fault or error lay in this, that they were wont to meet together on a stated day before it was light, and sing among themselves

alternately a hymn to Christ, as a god, and
bind themselves by an oath, not to the commission of any wickedness, but not to be
guilty of theft, or robbery, or adultery, never
to falsify their word, nor to deny a pledge
committed to them, when called upon to
return it. When these things were per-
formed, it was their custom to separate, and
then to come together again to a meal which
they ate in common, without any disorder;
but this they had foreborne since the publication of my edict, by which, according to
your commands, I prohibited assemblies.

"After receiving this account, I judged it
the more necessary to examine, and that by
torture, two maid-servants, which were called
ministers. But I have discovered nothing
beside a bad and excessive superstition.
Suspending therefore all judicial proceedings,
I have recourse to you for advice; for it has
appeared unto me a matter highly deserving
consideration, especially upon account of the
great number of persons who are in danger
of suffering. For many of all ages, and

every rank, of both sexes likewise, are accused, and will be accused. Nor has the contagion of this superstition seized cities only, but the lesser towns also, and the open country. Nevertheless, it seems to me that it may be restrained and corrected. It is certain that the temples, which were almost forsaken, begin to be more frequented. And the sacred solemnities, after a long intermission, are revived. Victims likewise are everywhere bought up, whereas for some time there were few purchasers. Whence it is easy to imagine what numbers of men might be reclaimed, if pardon were granted to those who shall repent."

These two documents are of intense interest. They give us a view from outside of what we are accustomed to see from inside. They make us sure of the following facts: that not many years had passed after the death of Christ under Pontius Pilate before a great multitude of people in various parts of the world (from its great centre Rome to distant provinces) had become disciples of the Lord

Jesus; that they were greatly scorned and hated for doing so; that though they really lived harmless and religious lives, they were accused of atheism, misanthropy, and obstinacy; that fierce and cruel persecutions were inflicted on them to make them renounce their religion and revile the person they called Christ; but that vast numbers of them suffered torture and death rather than fail in their loyalty to this Christ.

Apparently by chance these two documents from that remote antiquity are preserved among the remnants of classic literature. Not until comparatively recent years was any notice taken of them. And now by their unconscious witness they bring us to a standpoint close to the period during which the apostles laboured, and let us see, even through the eyes of her enemies, the Church of Christ carrying on in that early age her brave battle against heathenism. It is as if out of a pile of old newspapers from a distant land we had found two which contained as matter of every-day gossip the adventures of some dear friend of whose history we were longing to know the details.

Turning now from this outside view of the Christian Church, in which it appears as an unpopular, despised, persecuted, and yet very steadfastly determined body of people, pressing on its own way of life in spite of every opposition, let us look for a while at the view from within, and study the picture of the Church's life drawn for us by the writings of her own members. I think I ought to mention first a brief writing, not on parchment but on stone, which in harmony yet in strange contrast with the heathen notices of the persecuted religion, comes to us as a testimony from a silent city of the dead. Among the inscriptions in the long buried Roman catacombs is found the following from the reign of Hadrian, who succeeded Trajan, A.D. 117:

"In Christ. In the time of the emperor Adrian, Marius, a young military officer, who had lived long enough when with his blood he gave up his life for Christ. At length he rested in peace. The well-deserving set up this with tears and in fear on the 6th Ides of December" (Maitland's *Church in the Catacombs*).

The writing for which I next ask your attention is the latest in date of the series which we have to consider in this lecture. The *Shepherd of Hermas* is mentioned and quoted several times by writers in the latter part of the second century. Great reverence was paid to it on the supposition that the author was an "apostolic" Father. He was supposed to be the same as the Hermas mentioned by St. Paul in his letter to the Romans. The researches of modern criticism have shown this identity to be mistaken; yet from internal as well as external evidence we may conclude that he wrote very early in the second century, during the lifetime of the Clement whose letter we shall consider just now, and that he belonged to the sub-apostolic generation. His book is simple in style, very visionary and fanciful, but written with deep, earnest, and practical piety. He shows a firm belief in the great facts on which our faith rests. He speaks of the Lord Jesus always as the Son of God, implying continually Ilis Incarnation and the forgiveness of sins through His redemption. He is very familiar with persecution, and feels deeply the danger of denying the Lord Jesus, and the honour and blessedness of being steadfast for Him. Many passages of his book are reflections of the New Testament teaching, if not actual quotations from its writings. The *Shepherd of Hermas* is often called the *Pilgrim's Progress* of the early Church.

The following extracts will enable you to judge of its spirit :

" ' Why,' said I, ' is the Son of God, in this parable, put in the place of a servant ? ' ' Hearken,' said he. ' The Son of God is not put in the condition of a servant, but in great power and authority.' I said unto him, ' How, sir ? I understand it not.' ' Because,' said he, ' the Son set His messengers over those whom the Father delivered unto

Him, to keep every one of them ; but He
Himself laboured very much, and suffered
much, that He might blot out their offences.
For no vineyard can be digged without much
labour and pains. Wherefore, having blotted
out the sins of His people, He showed to
them the paths of life, giving them the law
which he had received of the Father.' . . .

"'First of all, sir,' said I, 'tell me what this
rock and this gate denote.' 'Hearken,' said
he. 'This rock and this gate are the Son
of God.' I replied, 'Sir, how can that be,
seeing the rock is old, but the gate new?'
'Hear,' said he, 'O foolish man, and understand. The Son of God is, indeed, more
ancient than any creature, insomuch that He
was in counsel with His Father at the crea-
tion of all things. But the gate is therefore
new, because He appeared in the last days
at the fulness of time ; that they who shall
attain unto salvation may by it enter into the
kingdom of God.' . . . 'No man shall
enter into the kingdom of God, but he who
shall take upon him the name of the Son of

God. For if you would enter into any city,
and that city should be encompassed with a
wall, and had only one gate, could you enter
into that city except by that gate?' I
answered, 'Sir, how could I do otherwise?'
'As therefore,' said he, 'there would be no
other way of entering into that city but by
its gate, so neither can any one enter into the
kingdom of God, but only by the name of
His Son, who is most dear unto Him.' He
added, 'Whosoever therefore shall not take
upon him His name, he shall not enter into
the kingdom of God.' . . . 'Why then,
sir, have all these fruit, indeed, but yet some
fairer than others?' 'Hearken,' said he.
'Whosoever have suffered for the name of the
Lord are esteemed honourable by the Lord ;
and all their offences are blotted out, because
they have suffered death for the name of the
Son of God. Hear now why their fruits are
different, and some of them excel others.
They who, being brought before magistrates,
and being asked, denied not the Lord, but
suffered with a ready mind, these are more

honourable with the Lord. The fruits, therefore, that are the most fair, are these. But
they who were fearful and doubtful, and have
deliberated with themselves whether they
should confess or deny Christ, and yet have
suffered, their fruits are smaller, because that
this thought came into their hearts. For it
is a wicked and evil thought for a servant
to deliberate whether he should deny his
master. . . . But ye who suffer death for
His name's sake ought to honour the Lord,
that He has esteemed you worthy to bear
His name, and that you should be delivered
from all your sins. And why, therefore, do
you not rather esteem yourselves happy ? '
. . . I said unto her, ' Lady, I would
know what it is that they have suffered ? '
' Hear then,' said she : ' wild beasts, scourg-
ings, imprisonments, and crosses, for His
name's sake. For this cause, the right hand
of holiness belongs to them, and to all others,
as many as shall suffer for the name of
God.' . . .

"Abstain not from any good works, but do

them. 'Hear,' said he, 'what the interior of those good works is which thou must do, that thou mayest be saved. The first of all is faith, the fear of the Lord, charity, concord, equity, truth, patience, chastity. There is nothing better than these things in the life of man, who shall keep and do things in their life. Hear next what follow these. To minister to the widows, not to despise the fatherless and poor; to redeem the servants of God from necessity; to be hospitable (for in hospitality there is sometimes great fruit); not to be contentious, but be quiet; to be humble above all men; to reverence the aged; to labour to be righteous; to respect the brotherhood; to bear affront, to be long-suffering; not to cast away those that have fallen from the faith, but to convert them, and make them be of good cheer; to admonish sinners; not to oppress those that are our debtors; and all other things of a like kind.' "

I call your attention next to the epistle of Polycarp, Bishop of Smyrna, addressed to the

Philippians. The most searching criticism has made us sure of the genuineness of this precious old letter. It was written shortly after the martyrdom of Ignatius, Bishop of Antioch, the date of which is fixed by Bishop Lightfoot, on the most carefully stated ground, at about A.D. 110. Polycarp was born about A.D. 70, and was himself martyred by fire in extreme old age, c. A.D. 155. The great writer, Irenæus, about A.D. 180, speaks of him thus : "I can tell the very place where the blessed Polycarp used to sit when he discoursed ; . . . and the discourses which he held before the people, and how he would describe his intercourse with John and with the rest of those who had seen the Lord, and how he would relate their words. And whatsoever things he had heard from them about the Lord, and about His miracles, and about His teaching, Polycarp, as having received them from eye-witnesses of the life of the Word, would relate altogether in accordance with the Scriptures."

Let me read you two or three sentences

written by this venerable man, who in his youth listened to St. John and other companions of our Lord.

"Polycarp and the presbyters that are with him unto the Church of God which sojourneth at Philippi ; Mercy unto you and peace from God Almighty and Jesus Christ our Saviour be multiplied.

1. "I rejoiced with you greatly in our Lord Jesus Christ, for that ye received the followers of the true Love and escorted them on their way, as befitted you—those men encircled in saintly bonds which are the diadems of them that be truly chosen of God and our Lord ; and that the steadfast root of your faith which was famed from primitive times abideth until now and beareth fruit unto our Lord Jesus Christ, who endured to face even death for our sins, whom God raised, having loosed the pangs of Hades ; on whom, though ye saw Him not, ye believe with joy unutterable and full of glory ; unto which joy many desire to enter in ; forasmuch as ye know that it is by grace

ye are saved, not of works, but by the will of God through Jesus Christ.

2. "Wherefore gird up your loins and serve God in fear and truth, forsaking the vain and empty talking and the error of the many, for that ye have believed on Him that raised our Lord Jesus Christ from the dead, and gave unto Him glory and a throne on His right hand ; unto whom all things were made subject that are in heaven and that are on the earth ; to whom every creature that hath breath doeth service, who cometh as judge of quick and dead ; whose blood God will require of them that are disobedient unto Him. Now He that raised Him from the dead will raise us also ; if we do His will and walk in His commandments and love the things which He loved, abstaining from all unrighteousness, covetousness, love of money, evil speaking, false witness ; not rendering evil for evil or railing for railing.

8. "Let him therefore without ceasing hold fast by our hope, and by the earnest of our righteousness, which is Jesus Christ, who took

up our sins in His own body upon the tree, who did no sin, neither was guile found in His mouth, but for our sakes He endured all things, that we might live in Him. Let us therefore become imitators of His endurance ; and if we should suffer for His name's sake, let us glorify Him. For He gave this example to us in His own person, and we believed this.

9. " I exhort you all therefore to be obedient unto the word of righteousness, and to practise all endurance, which also ye saw with your own eyes in the blessed Ignatius and Zosimus and Rufus, yea, and in others also who came from among yourselves, as well as in Paul himself and the rest of the apostles ; being persuaded that all these ran not in vain, but in faith and righteousness, and that they are in their due place in the presence of the Lord, with whom also they suffered. For they loved not the present world, but Him that died for our sakes and was raised by God for us.

12. " For I am persuaded that ye are well

trained in the sacred writings, and nothing is hidden from you. But to myself this is not granted. Only, as it is said in these Scriptures, Be ye angry and sin not, and let not the sun set on your wrath. Blessed is he that remembereth this ; and I trust that this is in you. Now may the God and Father of our Lord Jesus Christ, and the eternal High Priest Himself, the God Jesus Christ, build you up in faith and truth, and in all gentleness, and in all avoidance of wrath, and in forbearance and long suffering, and in patient endurance and in purity; and may He grant unto you a lot and portion among His saints, and to us with you, and to all that are under heaven, who shall believe on our Lord and God Jesus Christ and on His Father, that raised Him from the dead. Pray for all the saints. Pray also for kings and powers and princes, and for them that persecute and hate you, and for the enemies of the Cross, that your fruit may be manifest among all men, that ye may be perfect in Him."

From the letter of Polycarp to the epistles of Ignatius we have only to go back a very short time. Ignatius wrote during the stages of his journey to martyrdom ; Polycarp almost immediately after that solemn event. But the testimony of Ignatius brings us thirty years nearer to the life of Christ. We have seven deeply interesting letters written by him. Bishop Lightfoot spent years of patient study in mastering all the evidence bearing on these precious relics of antiquity. He learned two difficult languages, Armenian and Coptic, so as to be able to read and weigh all the documents connected with the subject. I need not occupy your time by details as to the various forms under which the epistles have been preserved through the long centuries. It is sufficient to say that the seven letters gathered together in the shorter collection called the "Vossian" are genuine letters by Ignatius.

Archdeacon Farrar, in his recent work, *Lives of the Fathers*, gives an interesting note as to the manner in which the Syriac MSS.

of the letters of Ignatius were procured. "Archbishop Ussher, in his anxiety to throw light on the Ignatian controversy, had invoked the assistance of the Government; and the captains of vessels who traded in the Levant were ordered to bring home what MSS. they could. Then Mr. Huntington, a chaplain at Aleppo, tried to interest the Greek ecclesiastics in the matter, and in 1679 braved all difficulties and visited the Nitrian monasteries. He obtained some MSS., which he placed in the Bodleian. Assemani, going with a commission from Pope Clement XI., brought home from Nitria some four MSS., which are now in the Vatican. Lastly, in 1830, Archdeacon Tattan brought home forty more MSS., which are now in the British Museum."

Ignatius was born c. 40. Martyred c. 110. Very early tradition speaks of him as an apostolic man, one who had intercourse with St. Peter, St. Paul, and St. John. We can be sure, from the date of his birth, that he must have been a middle-aged man before

St. John died. A few extracts will show the
harmony of his teaching with that of the
apostles.

1. " I know both who I am, and to whom
I write : I, a person condemned ; ye, such as
have obtained mercy. I, exposed to danger ;
ye, confirmed against danger. Ye are the
passage of those that are killed for God, the
companions of Paul in the mysteries of the
gospel—the holy, the martyr, the deservedly
most happy Paul ; at whose feet may I be
found, when I shall have attained unto God ;
who throughout all his epistles makes mention of you in Christ Jesus : . . . of all
which nothing is hid from you, if ye have
perfect faith and charity in Christ Jesus,
which are the beginning and end of life ; for
the beginning is faith, the end charity. . . .

2. " For this cause did the Lord suffer the
ointment to be poured on His head, that
He might breathe the breath of immortality
into His Church. Be not ye therefore
anointed with the evil savour of the doctrine of the prince of this world ; let him not

take you captive from the life that is set
before you. And why are not we all wise,
seeing we have received the knowledge of
God, which is Jesus Christ? Why do we
suffer ourselves foolishly to perish, not considering the gift which the Lord has truly
sent to us? Let my life be sacrificed for the
doctrine of the Cross, which is indeed a
scandal to the unbelievers, but to us is salvation and life eternal. 'Where is the wise
man? Where is the disputer?' Where is
the boasting of them that are called wise?
For our Lord Jesus Christ was, according
to the dispensation of God, conceived in the
womb of Mary, of the seed of David, by the
Holy Ghost. He was born and baptized,
that through His passion He might purify
water 'to the washing away of sin.' . . .

3. "But if Jesus Christ shall give me grace
through your prayers, and if it be His will,
I purpose, in a second epistle, which I will
suddenly write unto you, to manifest to you
more fully the dispensation of which I have
now begun to speak, unto the new Man,

which is Jesus Christ; both in His faith and
charity, in His suffering and in His resurrection ; especially if the Lord shall make
known unto me, that ye all by name come
together in common in one faith, and in one
Jesus Christ (who was of the race of David
according to the flesh) the Son of man, and
Son of God ; obeying your bishop and pres-
bytery with an entire affection ; breaking
one and the same bread, which is the
medicine of immortality, our antidote that we
should not die, but live for ever in Christ
Jesus. . . .

4. "All the ends of the world, and the
kingdoms of it, will profit me nothing. I
would rather die for Jesus Christ, than ride
to the utmost ends of the earth. Him I
seek who died for us ; Him I desire who rose
again for us. This is the gain that is laid up
for me."

The epistle called the *Epistle of Clement*
had a great name and fame in the early
Church. It seems to have been in many
places read aloud in the Christian assemblies.

It is translated in the oldest version of the New Testament, the Syriac "Peshito," and comes after the canonical books in the Alexandrian MS. It is quoted by several succeeding writers in the second century. The epistle does not bear the name of Clement, but is sent in the name of the Church at Rome to the Church at Corinth. The latest date that can be assigned to it is A.D. 95 or 96, during the trying times of the reign of Domitian.

1. " Through zeal and envy, the most faithful and righteous pillars of the Church have been persecuted, even to the most grievous deaths. Let us therefore set before our eyes the holy apostles; Peter, by unjust envy, underwent, not one or two, but many sufferings, till at last, being martyred, he went to the place of glory that was due unto him. For the same cause did Paul in like manner receive the reward of his patience. Seven times he was in bonds; he was whipped, was stoned; he preached both in the East and in the West, leaving behind

him the glorious report of his faith ; and so having taught the whole world of righteousness, and for that end travelled even to the utmost bounds of the West, he at last suffered martyrdom, by the command of the governors, and departed out of the world, and went unto his holy place, being become a most eminent pattern of patience unto all ages. . . .

2. " Let us consider what is good, and acceptable, and well pleasing in the sight of Him that made us. Let us look steadfastly to the blood of Christ, and see how precious His blood is in the sight of God : which, being shed for our salvation, has obtained the grace of repentance for all the world. . . . .

3. " Let us consider, beloved, how the Lord does continually show us, that there shall be a future resurrection, of which He has made our Lord Jesus Christ the firstfruits, raising Him from the dead. Let us contemplate, beloved, the resurrection, that is continually made before our eyes. . . .

4. " This is the way, beloved, in which we may find our Saviour, even Jesus Christ, the High Priest of all our offerings, the Defender and Helper of our weakness. By Him we look up to the highest heavens, and behold as in a glass His spotless and most excellent visage. By Him are the eyes of our hearts opened ; by Him our foolish and darkened understanding rejoiceth to behold His wonderful light. By Him would God have us to taste the knowledge of immortality, ' who, being the brightness of His glory, is by so much greater than the angels as He has by inheritance obtained a more excellent name than they.' For so it is written, ' Who maketh His angels spirits, and His ministers a flame of fire.' But to His Son thus saith the Lord, ' Thou art My Son ; to-day have I begotten Thee.' ' Ask of Me, and I will give Thee the heathen for Thine inheritance, and the utmost parts of the earth for Thy possession.' And again He saith unto Him, ' Sit Thou on My right hand, until I make Thine enemies Thy foot-

stool.' But who are His enemies? Even
the wicked, and such as oppose their own
wills to the will of God. Let us therefore
march on, men and brethren, with all earnest-
ness in His holy laws. . . .

5. " For as God liveth, and the Lord Jesus
Christ liveth, and the Holy Spirit, the Faith,
and the Hope of the elect, so shall he who,
in lowliness of mind with steadfast meekness,
hath wrought without sorrow the judgments
and statutes which are given by God, even
he shall be enrolled and had in honour,
among the number of those who are saved
through Jesus Christ, by whom is glory to
Him for ever and ever. Amen."

One more sub-apostolic writing we have
to consider. It is called the *Epistle of
Barnabas.* It was received in parts of the
ancient Church with great reverence, was by
many looked upon as Scripture, under the
idea that it was written by Barnabas, the
companion of St. Paul. This idea, however,
does not seem to be well founded. Dr.
Salmon, after a careful review of all the

evidence, concludes that though there is un-certainty as to the authorship of the book, it was certainly written during the reign of Vespasian, shortly after the destruction of Jerusalem, A.D. 70–79. The antiquity of the document gives it a very deep interest. We find in it, as to reasoning and breadth of view, a sad decline from the apostolic tone. But a few extracts will show the firm grasp of our Christian creed held by this old writer, who hovered on the border be-tween the apostolic and sub-apostolic age.

1. " For this cause did our Lord vouchsafe to give up His body to destruction, that through the forgiveness of our sins we might be sanctified ; that is, by the sprinkling of His blood. Now, for what concerns the things that are written about Him—some belong to the people of the Jews, and some to us. For thus saith the Scripture, ' He was wounded for our transgressions, He was bruised for our iniquities, and by His blood we are healed. He was led as a lamb to the slaughter ; and as a sheep before his shearers

is dumb, so He opened not His mouth.'
Wherefore we ought the more to give thanks
unto God, for that He hath both declared
unto us what is past, and not suffered us
to be without understanding of those things
that are to come.   .   .   .

2. "Now, how He suffered for us, seeing
that it was by men that He underwent it,
I will show you. The prophets, having
received from Him the gift of prophecy,
spake before concerning Him ; but He, that
He might abolish death, and make known
the resurrection from the dead, was content,
as it was necessary to appear in the flesh,
that He might make good the promise
before given to our fathers ; and preparing
Himself a new people might demonstrate to
them, whilst He was upon earth, that after
the resurrection He would judge the world.
And finally, teaching the people of Israel,
and doing many wonders and signs among
them, He preached to them and showed
the exceeding great love which He bare
towards them.   And when He chose His

apostles, which were afterwards to publish His gospel, He took men who had been very great sinners, that thereby He might plainly show, 'That He came not to call the righteous, but sinners to repentance.' That He clearly manifested Himself to be the Son of God. For had He not come in the flesh, how could men have been able to look upon Him that they might be saved?

.   .   .

3. "Moses then himself, who had commanded them, saying, 'Ye shall not make to yourselves any graven or molten image to be your God,' yet now did so himself, that he might represent to them the figure of the Lord Jesus. For he made a brazen serpent, and set it up on high, and called the people together by a proclamation; where, being come, they entreated Moses that he would make an atonement for them, and pray that they might be healed. Then Moses spake unto them saying, 'When any one among you shall be bitten, let him come unto the serpent that is set upon the pole;

and let him assuredly trust in him that, though he be dead, yet he is able to give life, and presently he shall be saved'; and so they did. See therefore how here also you have in this the glory of Jesus ; 'and that in Him and to Him are all things.'"

There are some other curious relics of sub-apostolic literature, which, although our time would not allow us to consider closely, it is well we should be aware of. They are writings of "heretics," men who acknow-ledged Christ, but held views different from those of the main body of the Christian Church. Three of these wrote in the begin-ning of the second century—Basilides, Valen-tinus, and Marcion. In various ways a good deal of their writings has been preserved. Their views were visionary and extravagant. They speculated wildly about the origin of good and evil. But though they wove the gospel history into fantastic combination with their peculiar speculations, yet even amidst these curious minglings of fact and imagination, we see the same majestic figure of Jesus standing prominent, and the same general outline of His earthly history that we see in the writings of the orthodox.

Now let us try to put together in our minds the results that we gather from the writings we have been considering. They were all, both the heathen and the Christian documents, certainly written by men who were born before Christ's contemporaries had died. Some were written by men who had had in their early days personal intercourse with apostles of Christ. They give us a photograph of the society called the Christian Church at that early period. What do we see in the photograph? We see in the generation immediately succeeding that of Jesus of Nazareth a wide-spread society, bound together by a belief in certain definite facts about Him, animated by a deep devotion and reverence to Him, and striving to practise a very lofty morality for His sake.

We see among the scattered communities a close mutual connexion and a certain simple but effective organization. We see

an initiatory rite of baptism, a rite of breaking bread together in remembrance of their
Founder's death, and a regular government
by appointed teachers. We see that the
members looked back continually, for their
guidance in opinion and their inspiration in
life, to the teaching of the men who had been
companions of Jesus. They spoke of some
of them by name, and echoed in their exhortations to each other the sentiments which
we find in the writings of these earlier
teachers. Their faith made them fearless
in facing persecution, and produced among
them an ideal of what human life ought to
be, beautiful and holy beyond all that had
been dreamed of by poet or philosopher before the coming of Christ. But the most
important thing we see in these writings is,
that the faith held by the sub-apostolic
Church and the morality taught by her are
exactly the same as what was taught afterwards by an ever-widening series of well-
known writers through the second century,
and exactly the same as what is taught in the

documents which we believe have come to us from the apostles of Christ. Are our gospels reliable records of what the apostles witnessed? When they tell us of Christ's Life, teaching, miracles, Death, Resurrection, and Ascension, do they tell us what St. Peter, St. James, and St. John saw and declared? or do they tell us something that was afterwards made out? Certainly those Christians who were born before the apostles died believed that they had taught just as we believe now. All the statements, beliefs, and hopes of our gospels are re-echoed by these old Fathers. If our gospels were not current among them, as we have the strongest reason to believe they were, yet certainly what they believed about Jesus was just the same as our gospels declare.

Thus the sub-apostolic writers form a strong link, binding the Church as we know her distinctly through the voluminous, well-preserved writings we have in the latter half of the second century, with the Church of the apostles' times. As the years passed, and her branches

spread farther and farther, her doctrines took
a more carefully expressed dogmatic form,
her organization settled into more rigid lines;
but the picture of her Founder's character,
the gospel teaching to men's hearts and consciences, the belief in the facts of Christ's
history—all this as told by Irenæus in 180,
by Tatian in 160, by Justin Martyr in 140,
by Hermas in 120, by Polycarp in 112, by
Ignatius in 110, by Clement in 95, by Barnabas in 80—all this, I say, was exactly the
same as what was told by St. Paul, St. Peter,
St. Matthew, St. Mark, St. Luke, and St.
John, who took their teaching from the lips
of Jesus Himself, and from the lips of His
immediate companions. Whether the facts
happened or not, the belief that they had
happened, and the holy motives and happy
hopes that sprang from that belief, most
certainly continued in the Church without
variation from a few days after Jesus suffered
under Pontius Pilate till to-day. The value
of the sub-apostolic writings is, that they
supply an important link in the chain of

unaltering belief. When did this belief begin? When did it first appear? Through the old literature we hunt up from generation to generation, and we ask, Did it begin here? Did these men invent it? Did these men improve or develop it? But we have to answer as we turn up each old folio, Here is the belief, not beginning, not struggling into existence, but fully formed and firmly held, in spite of persecution and obloquy. Here is the belief in Christ crucified and risen; here is the belief in Christ still living as Saviour and King; here is the expectation of Christ to come again in judgment. Here is the creed, the same in its essence, in every scrap of evidence that can be found bearing on the early ages of Christianity; not the slightest indication of any other belief among Christians; not the slightest hint by any writer, whether orthodox or heterodox, through which we can trace the beginning of the belief to anything else than the actual facts of the story.

Thus is answered for us our most anxious

questioning. Is the religion preached in the name of Christ actually true? It is certainly beautiful. It is comforting in sorrow, strengthening in temptation, elevating in daily life: that we feel and know. It has certainly been, through the history of the world, a blessing and a joy to millions. But can we rely upon its statements as authentic history? We are satisfied that it was not a conscious fabrication. No one now holds such an idea. Those who taught such noble morality could not possibly have made statements in order to promulgate it which they knew to be false. And we are satisfied that the story about Christ dead and risen again was not a dreamy imagination. The rough touch of persecution would soon waken from sentimental reverie. The manifest good sense and practical wisdom that breathes through the apostolic writings makes it impossible to think that their authors were wild enthusiasts, imagining they had seen things they never saw, and heard words that had never been spoken.

But could this gospel story have been a gradual growth, by which the aspirations and longings of the human heart found for themselves a dramatic expression ideally true but literally false? This is the only possible solution of the phenomena before us if the gospel of Christ is not historically true. It is the favourite solution with unbelievers just now. But the literature we have been considering shows us that this solution is impossible. It shows, with a proof so clear as to be not only probable, but demonstrative, that there was no *growth* ever in the story of what Christ was and did. Never was there room or opportunity for it. We see from step to step, through the long past ages, the Church of Christ combined together with a certain deep conviction about Jesus of Nazareth as the reason for its existence. We walk round about her battlements and tell her towers, to see if we can find anywhere a place where a new story about Christ could have crept in. But, like sentinels carefully posted at intervals within hearing of each other, we find

these old Christian authors each testifying,
" There could have been no such entry here."
Irenæus, Justin, Papias, Hermas, Polycarp,
Ignatius, Barnabas, Clement, St. John, St.
Paul, they fill up all the time between Christ's
death and the period when Christianity was as
well known as it is now.   When could the new
ideas as to the Christian history have begun ?
When, from a holy and talented martyr, could
Christ have grown in the Church's mind to
be the Son of God, dead and risen again ?
When ?   Each of these sentinels stands forth
and says, " It was not in my time."   " We
received from our teachers the faith that we
believe to be the faith once for all delivered
to the saints.   We have been commanded that
if any one brought us any other gospel than
that which we have received, we are not to
bid him God-speed."   By every one of the
writers we have been considering Christ is
looked upon in the same light.   Later in the
Church's development indeed, there were
fierce disputes as to the nature of Christ,
and as to the relation of the Divine and

human in His Person ; even in the sub-apostolic age such questions began to be raised, and "heretics," as we said just now, interpreted His history in curious ways. They were inclined, not to develop the story, but to twist it in fanciful directions. But never was there a time during the lives of the apostles and those who immediately succeeded them when there was any opportunity of substituting our supernatural history for an originally natural one. Each step that we go back shows us the same picture of Jesus teaching as never man taught, performing works above all human power, crucified, risen from the grave, and worshipped by His people.

The only difference is (as we shall have to consider in our next lecture), that the picture is painted for us with more delicate skill and more lovely colours in the time of His contemporaries than in any succeeding age. What then must be our conclusion ?

This light, that shines so brightly on the gospel page—this light, that illumines the

sub-apostolic writings with such a soft and
pious glow—this light, that began in the
Life, Death, and Resurrection of Jesus, and
that has never since been quenched, is just
the light from heaven, God's light enlight-
ening the world.

Reason here agrees with feeling. Careful
search corroborates instinctive judgment.
There is no possibility of the story of Christ
having been altered before it reached us.
No ingenuity can find any dark, unknown
spot for its growth or change. From its
first birth it has been the same. Testified
to us by the men who knew the Lord Jesus,
who had heard His teaching, who had seen
Him dead, and seen Him risen—testified by
them at peril of death—testified along with
the most beautiful teaching to heart and
conscience —testified so that the echoes of
the story have rung through the world ever
since, and have brought with them strength
in life and hope in death wherever they have
been listened to : testified thus, how can we
possibly receive this story otherwise than

as a true history of what actually happened
—a history which an earlier writer than any
which I have yet quoted has thus epitomized:
"The Word was made flesh, and dwelt among
us ; and we beheld His glory, the glory as of
the only begotten of the Father"?

LECTURE II.

THE GRADUAL GROWTH OF THE NEW TESTAMENT CANON.

By Rev. CANON WYNNE, D.D.

LECTURE II.

THE GRADUAL GROWTH OF THE NEW TESTAMENT CANON.

DURING the reign of Diocletian, about the year A.D. 303, there broke out a terrible persecution against Christianity. For some time the Church had had rest. Now the fire of heathen wrath blazed up for a little while against the religion that was rapidly conquering it. The edict went forth, that Christian churches were to be razed to the ground and Christian books were to be burned. The former persecutions had been directed against persons; this attack was levelled, not only against persons, but against books. Eusebius, the great historian of the early Church, thus describes the scenes of which he was an eye-witness:

"I saw with my own eyes the houses of prayer thrown down and razed to their foundations, and the inspired and sacred Scriptures consigned to fire in the open market place." Out of that time of trial and danger for the Christian community there arose a phrase which carried with it important instruction for future ages—the phrase " canonical Scriptures." When Christians were pressed on pain of torture and death to give up their sacred books, the question arose, which might they lawfully give up, and which was it imperative on them to keep? Those who gave up the Scriptures were looked on by their fellow Christians as " traditores," traitors who had basely yielded up what they ought to have treasured as dearer than life. But all their books were not equally sacred. Some were good and instructive ; but some were much more than this, they contained the teaching of Christ's apostles. They had come straight from the fountain of truth. They were the guides of their faith and of their lives. The distinction had long been known and understood. But now the stern edict of heathen authority made it more important to have a definite " canon," or rule, by which timid Christians could be guided so as to be sure of the difference between good books and inspired books. Bitter controversies arose after that time as to the treatment of those who had been " traditores "; and from the heat of those controversies the expression " canonical " issued as a general title for the apostolic writings. The word " canon " or " straight rule " had been used before with regard to right doctrine ; from the Diocletian persecution and the controversies with the Donatists it came to be used with regard to the books that were accepted by the Church as rightly belonging to the New Testament. Our task in this paper is to trace the growth of the idea expressed by the word " canon " from a general consciousness to a distinct registration.

I shall try to lay before you in a brief

sketch the history of the facts we know
on the subject, and then to show you their
bearing on the evidences for Christianity.

I. As we considered the writings of the
second century, though we recognised their
identity, both in spiritual tone and doctrinal
teaching, with the writings of the apostolic
age, we noticed at the same time a great
difference. They are marvellously inferior
to the older writings. They do not at all
approach to the breadth, depth, clearness,
and dignity of the literature from which they
have drawn so much, and which in a feeble
way they re-echo. Amidst much that is
precious and true, we see painful signs of
narrow prejudices, and of the almost childish
ways of reasoning and interpreting books,
prevalent at the time. The difference between the apostolic and the sub-apostolic
writings is something like the difference
between a nugget of pure gold and a block
of quartz with veins of the precious metal
gleaming through it. If we had to judge now
by literary tests between the New Testament

writings and all others that have come down to us from the early ages of Christianity ; if we had to judge which were most fitted to lead and mould human thought, which had least that was merely ephemeral and local, and most that was enduring and universal in their teaching,—I am certain that we should be forced to choose the very books that were gradually gathered together and set apart by the early Church in its canon of inspired Scripture. Still, it was not by literary tests, but by knowledge of facts that the Church chose. How their verdict was decided we have to consider.

We must put aside speculation as to how we might think it likely a revelation would be given. The way it was given has not that complete and ready-made systematic form which we might have thought most convenient. Bishop Butler has shown from the analogy of nature how different from what might have been expected is the way the infinite and all-seeing God distributes His most precious gifts. Sensationalism and suddenness are generally alien from nature's processes. The great thing is to recognise the blessing and use it, though the way it came to us may not be what we should have looked for. It is hard to describe the first beginnings of the New Testament.

> "Who ever saw the earliest rose
> First open her sweet breast?
> Or, when the summer sun goes down,
> The first soft star in evening's crown
> Light up her gleaming crest?"

So appeared that flower which has filled the earth with its fragrance, that star which has guided upwards for centuries the weary feet of humanity. It came not with observation.

The New Testament began its course in the solemn yet wonderfully fruitful period immediately after the Resurrection of Christ and the descent of the great Pentecostal gift. The apostles went forth everywhere "preaching Christ." They were joined by zealous coadjutors who shared their convictions.

They went out first through Palestine and

Syria, then by degrees farther and farther into all the regions of the world as it was known at that time. The original form of their instructions was oral. They "preached the word." We rather shrink from the word "tradition," on account of the false ideas that have gathered round the term. But though we should be thankful for the security given to us by God's providence in the written word, which cannot change, yet the beginning of the New Testament was certainly *the apostolic tradition*—that which was handed on by the apostles from place to place and from Church to Church in their oral teaching. It was, as the writer of the Epistle to the Hebrews describes it, "the great salvation, which began to be spoken by the Lord, and was confirmed unto us by them that heard it."

In the three synoptic gospels, St. Matthew, St. Mark, and St. Luke, there are great general similarities, and yet continual differences. They come evidently from some common source, and yet not (as is suggested

by many considerations) a common written
source. Their relations one to another, their
agreements and disagreements, can best be
accounted for by supposing a common basis
of oral teaching. This is like a key that fits
and runs through complicated wards, and so
is judged to be the right key. In those first
few years the apostles, expecting the Lord's
immediate return and the consummation
of all things, had probably no intention to
write histories of Christ. They did the duty
that lay nearest to them, and preached the
kingdom of heaven. The providence of God
made a use of their preaching that they had
probably not foreseen. In oral teaching, not
in writing, their busy lives were spent. Their
first preaching was almost necessarily in
great part historical. They had important
facts to narrate. They had a splendid story
to unfold. So, in choosing a successor to the
fallen Judas, the essential qualification was
acquaintance with the facts of Christ's life
from the first ; and the early discourses of
St. Peter and St. John related in the Acts

are plain declarations of the miracles, Death, and Resurrection of Christ. Now this kind of teaching would naturally fall before long into somewhat of a customary form and order. The same story having to be continually told, would come to be told again and again in something of the same way. Certain parts of our Lord's life and teaching would come to be most often dwelt on. His Death and Resurrection would always be especially put forward. They formed the great basis of faith, so that whatever else had to be abbreviated or left out, sufficient time had always to be reserved for telling the whole story of the betrayal, crucifixion, and resurrection of the Lord. Details of the history would be varied by different persons and in different places ; but always the teaching would lead up to Calvary and the empty grave. So we have here, most probably, as far as we can judge by careful consideration of the likenesses and differences between them, the common basis of our synoptic gospels. We think of the various scenes

5

where the apostles preached : courts of the Jewish Temple, steps of Roman fortresses, the pillared porticoes of Grecian halls, guest-chambers in the houses of friends, upper rooms upon the third loft, shady spots beside flowing rivers—we think of the companions of Christ telling the old old story in such places, telling it over and over again, telling what they had seen and heard, telling others to tell the same. We think of little companies gathered together in villages and scattered houses as well as in great cities, repeating to one another what they had drunk in from the startling addresses of the apostles, we think of parents teaching the story to their children, and companies who were being made ready for baptism prepared and questioned in the same narrative. Thus began the collection and the order of apostolic teaching. St. Paul said to the Corinthians (probably before St. Matthew and St. Luke were written), that he had " delivered to them what he had received," and it is almost word for word the same as is written in the gospels he had never seen. He earnestly calls upon Timothy to keep the " deposit " which was committed to him, evidently meaning the sacred treasure of true facts, which he was to hold pure and unmixed with " profane and vain babblings."

St. Luke tells us that " many took in hand to draw up a narrative of the things that were fulfilled among us, even as they delivered them to us who were from the first eye-witnesses and ministers of the Word." He himself wrote " in order " to Theophilus, that he might know the certainty of those things wherein he had been " catechised."

Affection gradually strove to gather together and preserve in writing the teaching that had fallen from inspired lips. By these efforts the providence of God prepared the materials for the histories of St. Matthew, St. Mark, and St. Luke. The histories were all the outcome of the apostles' witness. One of the histories has been considered from the earliest age to have been put together by an apostle's hand.

St. John's gospel was different. It was written by one who had survived the first struggling into the light of the new religion. It was written with a special teaching object, by one who had been favoured with the intimate friendship of our Lord.

Perhaps the earliest written parts of the New Testament were letters—St. Paul's letters to the Churches he had founded, or in which he was deeply interested. Letters to individuals under special circumstances followed, or letters by other apostles or apostolic men, received with reverence and attention, and soon made the common property of the whole Christian society. A beautiful book describing the early history of the apostles, written by a companion of St. Paul, the compiler of one of the gospels, appeared about the same time, and then the grand though mystic Apocalypse, handed down to us by the last surviving apostle of Christ.

It is interesting to notice, that most of the New Testament books arose out of special circumstances, or were connected with special difficulties which the disciples of Christ were going through, or out of special occurrences among them. A great sin on the part of the member of one Church ; a collection for poor Christians in a crowded city ; the return of a runaway slave — incidents like these formed the immediate cause for the writing of letters that are a blessing and strength to Christ's people under all circumstances still. Thus a reality and life-like character are given to writings which God's providence prepared for the guidance of His people in every-day life. Certain controversies, too, which have now subsided or entirely changed their form, leave their traces deep on the apostolic letters. So, as in Miriam's song of triumph after the overthrow of the Egyptians, we have in our daily reading reminders of the struggles, dangers, and victories through which in times past our brethren have been led.

None of these New Testament books were ushered in as books are now by publishers, by advertisements, by public announcements.

They came as the violets come, springing up
quietly in their due season, recognised by the
fragrance they shed around them. That they
did appear, that they were gathered and treasured by the Christian community is made
certainly known to us by the way they are
mentioned in the literature of succeeding ages.

II. This brings us to the second part of our
subject. So far we have been thinking of
the *production* of the New Testament books.
Now we have to think of their reception.

In the age we were considering a short
time ago—the sub-apostolic—the traces of
the knowledge and reception of the New
Testament books are of a most interesting
character. By their very unconsciousness,
their absence of design in any way to mark
or stamp the inspired books, they bear them
the most reliable kind of testimony. The
idea of any special canon or catalogue of
books had not yet arisen.

While some of the writers were still living,
while in many of the Churches echoes of their
living voices were still ringing, people had

not thought of collecting and classifying their
writings. They were circulating—slowly for
the reasons I described in our last lecture—
but with a quiet and steady advance through
the Church. Handed on from one city to
another; read and re-read, and feasted on
evidently by loving disciples in every direction, their influence was forming the Church
before it had time to realize the treasure it
possessed in them. The New Testament
books are seldom directly and accurately
quoted by the sub-apostolic authors. They
treat them much as they treat the Old
Testament Scriptures. They embody their
thoughts, using their words, sometimes as
if quoted from memory, sometimes as if
they were so familiar with them that their
own thoughts naturally clothed themselves
in almost identical language. With regard
to the synoptic gospels, it is hard to be sure
whether they are reproducing their words
slightly altered by memory quotations, or
whether rather their ideas and knowledge
about the facts of Christ's history were formed

on the same apostolic round of oral teaching which constituted the basis of those three gospels.

With regard to the epistles, it is quite plain that they were familiar with a great many of them. I give you a few extracts from the writings of Clement, A.D. 95, and Polycarp, A.D. 112, in which you will recognise the evident presence of New Testament thoughts and the close similarity to New Testament words of which we have been speaking.

" Ye were kind one to another, without grudging, being ready to every good work."

" Let us consider what is good, and acceptable, and well-pleasing in the sight of Him that made us."

" Abraham, who was called God's friend, was in like manner found faithful, inasmuch as he obeyed the commands of God."

" Above all, remembering the words of the Lord Jesus, which He spake concerning equity and long suffering, saying, ' Be ye merciful, and ye shall obtain mercy ; forgive, and ye shall be forgiven ; as ye do, so shall

it be done unto you ; as ye give, so shall it
be given unto you ; as ye judge, so shall ye
be judged ; as ye are kind to others, so shall
God be kind to you ; with what measure ye
mete, with the same shall it be measured to
you again.' "

"Let that be far from us which is written :
' Miserable are the double-minded, and those
who are doubtful in their hearts.' "

" ' For God,' saith he, ' resisteth the proud,
but giveth grace to the humble.' "

" By Him are the eyes of our hearts opened ;
by Him our foolish and darkened understanding rejoiceth to behold His wonderful light."

" ' Who, being the brightness of His glory,
is by so much greater than the angels as He
has by inheritance obtained a more excellent
name than they.' For so it is written, ' Who
maketh His angels spirits, and His ministers
a flame of fire.' But to His Son, thus saith
the Lord, ' Thou art My Son, to-day have I
begotten Thee.' ' Ask of Me, and I will give
Thee the heathen for Thine inheritance, and
the utmost parts of the earth for Thine

inheritance.' And again He saith unto Him, 'Sit Thou on My right hand, until I make Thine enemies Thy footstool.'"

"So likewise our apostles knew, by our Lord Jesus Christ, that there should contentions arise upon account of the ministry."

"Wherefore are there strifes, and anger, and divisions, and schisms, and wars among us? Have we not all one God and one Christ? Is not one spirit of grace poured out among us all? Have we not one calling in Christ?"

"Remember the words of the Lord Jesus, how He said, 'Woe to that man (by whom offences came)! It were better for him that he had never been born, than that he should have offended one of My elect. It were better for him that a millstone should be hanged about his neck, and he should be cast into the sea, than that he should offend one of My little ones.'"

"As also that the root of the faith, which was preached from ancient times, remains firm in you to this day, and brings forth fruit to our Lord Jesus Christ, who suffered Him-

self to be brought even to the death for our
sins, 'whom God hath raised up, having
loosed the pains of death': 'whom, having
not seen ye love; in whom, though now ye
see Him not, yet believing, ye rejoice with
joy unspeakable, and full of glory'; into
which many desire to enter, knowing that
'by grace ye are saved,' not by works, but
by the will of God, through Jesus Christ."

"'Believing in Him that raised up our
Lord Jesus from the dead, and hath given
Him glory,' and a throne at His right hand;
to whom all things are made subject, 'both
that are in heaven, and that are in earth.'"

"Abstaining from all unrighteousness,
'inordinate affection, and love of money,
from evil speaking, false witness; not rendering evil for evil, railing for railing,' or
striking for striking, or cursing for cursing;
but remembering what the Lord has taught
us saying, 'Judge not, and ye shall not be
judged; forgive, and ye shall be forgiven.
Be ye merciful, and ye shall obtain mercy;
for with the same measure that ye mete

withal, it shall be measured to you again.'
And again, ' Blessed are the poor, and they
that are persecuted for righteousness sake :
for theirs is the kingdom of God.'"

"But 'the love of money is the root of
all evil.' Knowing therefore that, as 'we
brought nothing into this world, so neither
may we carry anything out,' 'let us arm
ourselves with the armour of righteousness.'
For 'whosoever does not confess that Jesus
Christ is come in the flesh, he is antichrist.'"

"Let us return to the word that was
delivered to us from the beginning : 'watch-
ing unto prayer,' and persevering in fasting ;
with supplication beseeching the all-seeing
God 'not to lead us into temptation,' as the
Lord hath said, ' The spirit truly is willing,
but the flesh is weak.'"

"Being kind and gentle towards each
other, despising none. When it is in your
power to do good, defer it not ; for 'charity
delivereth from death.' 'Be all of you subject one to another, having your conversation honest among the Gentiles' ; that by

your good works, both ye yourselves may
receive praise, and the Lord may not 'be
blasphemed through you.'"

In the next half century of early Christian history we have evidence of a rich and
voluminous literature having been produced.
But the greater part of it has perished,
leaving us only the names of various writers,
the subjects on which they wrote, and some
fragments, large or small, of their works.
One of the earliest and most prolific writers
of this time was Papias, a friend of Polycarp's. He was Bishop of Hierapolis, in
Phrygia, early in the second century. Fragments of his many and important writings
have been preserved for us in the history
of Eusebius. He is the first extant writer
who gives us the names of the authors of
two of our gospels in a document dating
about A.D. 130.

"Matthew," Papias said, "wrote the oracles
in the Hebrew tongue, and every one interpreted them as he was able." "Mark, as the
interpreter of Peter, wrote down accurately,

though not in order, all that he remembered
that was said or done by Christ. For he
neither heard the Lord nor attended on
Him, but later as I said, upon Peter, who
taught according to the occasion, and not
as composing a connected narrative of the
Lord's discourses ; so that Mark made no
mistake in writing down some things as he
remembered them. For he took care of one
thing, not to omit any of the particulars that
he heard, or to falsify any part of them."

About the same time as Papias lived
one of the most important of our early
Christian witnesses—Justin Martyr. He appears to have been born before the close of
the first century, and to have been martyred
between A.D. 160 and A.D. 170. His principal writings date from c. 140 to c. 150.
Three alone out of many have reached us—
two apologies and the *Dialogue with Trypho.* He quotes much as the elder writers
do, inexactly and without reference, just as
he quotes the Old Testament. The repro-
ductions of the gospel story in his writings

are so numerous, that it has been calculated
that if all our synoptic gospels were lost,
a history of Christ substantially the same as
theirs could be reconstructed out of Justin's
writings. Besides this, he expressly mentions
over and over again what he calls the
"Memoirs of the Apostles," in which he
found written "all things concerning Jesus
Christ." In describing the Lord's Supper,
for example, he says, "The apostles, in
the memoirs made by them, handed down
that it was thus enjoined to them." In the
graphic picture he draws of the Christian
services of his day, he mentions that the
"memoirs of the apostles or writings of the
prophets are read as long as time permits."

Written a little later than Justin's book,
there has come down to us a document to
which was given at some time the inaccurate
title of the Second Epistle of Clement. It
was not written by the same author or in
the same generation as the anonymous letter
called the First Epistle of Clement. It cannot, however, bear a later date than the middle

of the second century. The author of it uses our gospels and several of our epistles in the same way as Justin does, reproducing the ideas of the New Testament writers, and clothing his thoughts in language that is evidently an echo from theirs. He speaks of the Scriptures under the title of "The Books of the Apostles." After quoting a passage of Isaiah with the same application of it as is made by St. Paul, he continues, "Moreover another Scripture saith, I came not to call righteous men, but sinners."

In several other writers, some orthodox and some heterodox, about the same time, the middle of the second century and a little after, we see the same thing—evidence that their doctrines were formed on apostolic teaching, and that as apostolic they knew and used the writings that we read to-day.

A further development now begins to show itself—a desire to express which are the real apostolic books, and to guard against un-authorized intruders. Strange to say, the first appearance of a list of New Testament writings that we can lay our hands on is in the work of a heretic. The fact of his having made one for the use of his followers leads us to suppose that there were in existence others of which he disapproved. Marcion, one of the principal early second century heretics, formed a collection of sacred books as the ground and test of his teaching. It consists of two parts, the "gospel" and "the apostolicon." The gospel was that of St. Luke, with its text somewhat tampered with. The apostolicon consisted of ten epistles of St. Paul. Somewhat later than this, dating perhaps between A.D. 160 and 170, we find a list of books generally accepted by the Christian Church. It is called the Muratorian Fragment. It was discovered in the Ambrosian Library at Milan, by Muratori, during the seventeenth century. There is reason to believe that it was brought to Milan from the old Irish monastery of Bobbio. It is only a fragment. The beginning and end of it are torn away and lost. It begins with a broken sentence, which evidently refers to the position of St. Mark's gospel. The

writer goes on to say that "the gospel according to St. Luke stands third in order, having
been written by Luke the physician, the companion of St. Paul." The fourth place is
given to the gospel of St. John, a disciple of
the Lord. He then says, "Though various
ideas are taught in each of the gospels,
it makes no difference to believers, since in
all of them all things are declared by one
sovereign Spirit concerning the Nativity, the
Passion, the Resurrection, the conversation
[of our Lord] with His disciples, and His
double advent, first in humble guise, which
has taken place, and afterwards in royal
power, which is still future." The writer next
mentions the Acts, and thirteen epistles of
St. Paul. After this he treats of books which
are in circulation, but which, he says, "cannot be received into the Catholic Church ;
for gall cannot be mingled with honey." But
he mentions the Epistle of Jude, and 2nd
John, and the Apocalypse of John, and Peter.
"The latter," he says, "some of our body will
not have read in the church." The document

is a translation. The writing is very fragmentary, and the text imperfect. But the author states, not his own individual opinion, but the knowledge and practice of the Catholic Church. Thus we see emerging from the misty morning clouds of that early age a catalogue of books received as apostolic, received as inspired. It is, on the whole, the same catalogue as we have to-day, though a few of our books were not yet quite universally known and recognised in the Church, and one or two still hovered on the edge of the holy ground of canonicity, which the research and fuller knowledge of the next generation excluded.

Another step we can mark in the progress of the canon, amidst the dim shadows, is the making of versions. Two have come down to us from the second century. First, the ancient Syriac " Peshito," or simple translation, as it is called. There are many difficulties in identifying its first form and the date of its appearance. But we may safely conclude that it was made in the earlier half of the second century, that it had a very wide circulation, that it included our present books with the exception of 2nd and 3rd John, 2nd Peter, Jude, and the Apocalypse, with regard to which books there were considerable differences of opinion in the early ages.

Secondly, the "old Latin," also called a Peshito or simple version, may have been made a few years later. But it was used by Tertullian, who began to write about A.D. 190. It was an old and long-used version in his time. Twenty years would bring it back to 170, which is the latest date that could with any probability be assigned to it. Putting these two ancient versions together as representing the united witness of the East and West, we find shortly after the middle of the second century, treasured up, translated, and passed on from Church to Church as apostolic and inspired, all the books of our New Testament with the exception of 2nd Peter, and none but those which we acknowledge.

About the third quarter of this same second century appeared a remarkable document, on which one of the lecturers who is to follow me has written a valuable treatise. I refer to Tatian's *Diatessaron*, i.e. " By the four." It is a kind of synopsis or harmony of the four gospels, and was widely used for public reading in the Syrian Churches. Though Tatian was the leader of a heretical sect, yet the materials out of which the *Diatessaron* was composed are the four gospels received by the Church Catholic.

And now we emerge out of the clouds and come into the clear daylight of well-defined history. At the close of the second century several voluminous and brilliant writers flourished in the Church, and from this time forward Christian authors were so able and so numerous, and the Christian community became such an important factor in human history, that it is easy to know her ideas and her beliefs.

Irenæus was brought up in Asia Minor, and became bishop of Lyons in Gaul about A D.

177, succeeding the aged Pothinus, who was born ten or fifteen years before the end of the first century. At the same time we have the well-known *Clement of Alexandria*, the Latin Father *Tertullian* in the Church of Carthage, North Africa, and the noble and zealous *Origen*, "adamantine," as has been well said, in his courage, and unrivalled in his universal learning and his deep study of the Scriptures old and new.

From the time of these writers to the time of Eusebius, in the reign of Diocletian, the history of the canon may best be described through the phraseology Eusebius uses. He describes three classes of books. First, the acknowledged; second, the disputed; third, the spurious. At the close of the second century, what he calls the acknowledged books had been all generally recognised in the Church as apostolic. They were the four gospels, thirteen epistles of St. Paul, 1st John, and 1st Peter.

There were others which he classed as *disputed*, 2nd and 3rd John, Jude, Hebrews, 2nd

Peter, and strange to say, a book that was quoted by the very earliest writers—the Apocalypse. At the close of the second century, these were known and acknowledged in some parts of the Church, doubted or not mentioned in others. With the progress of inter-communion between the Churches in the third century, all these gradually became known, their claims to canonicity were understood, and they became by degrees more and more generally received as genuine and apostolic. A number of other books there were, some of them (like the *Shepherd of Hermas*) pious and genuine, but not apostolic; some of them dishonest endeavours by heretics to strengthen their opinions by honoured names. These, at the close of the second century, were classified as Scripture by some writers, disowned or ignored by others. The progress of knowledge and reasonable criticism in the third century was to put them all aside.

Thus the acknowledged books were all preserved, the needlessly doubted were established, and the spurious were rejected. And at the time when a definite canon had to be drawn up during the Diocletian persecution, the list of inspired books had been long fully formed, and weeded of unauthorized intruders. Thus, at the General Council of Nicæa, A.D. 325, the New Testament, as we have it to-day, was the basis of all argument

III. Having thus far considered together the production of the New Testament books, their reception into the Christian community, and the jealous care taken lest any not really apostolic should creep in among them, we are in a position to see how these facts bear on our Christian faith. We have observed how first there was belief in Christ, then the preached word about Christ, and then gradually the written word about Him. The word sprang from the belief, and then perpetuated and guided the belief. By the belief, so preserved and made known, the Church was formed and gathered together, and the Church in her turn became the witness and keeper of the teaching by which her faith was guided.

Thus our study leads us to two results—to be cautious as to the foundation of our faith, and yet to be sure of it.

The caution is, that we are not to consider our faith to rest on a book, but on a Person. Christ Himself, the Rock of ages, is the foundation. Our belief in Christ does not rest upon the inspiration of the New Testament, but our belief in that inspiration rests on our belief in Christ. Various converging arguments make us sure that the history of Christ's career and teaching told in the New Testament is not invented, not imagined, not developed, but actually true. This conclusion is independent of our belief in the inspiration of the books. We take the New Testament writers first merely as witnesses. We trace up the unbroken line of testimony to what Christians believed till we find it originated in the witness of Christ's companions, who told, at peril of life, what they had seen and heard. Through this witness we are led to believe in the supernatural character of His teaching and work. We are not affected in this belief by any supposed defect in the apostolic writings. Even if we could not reconcile all the details of their statements one with another, even if we did not agree with every sentiment they expressed, still we feel that their evidence is reliable, is irresistible. They could not have been deceived about what they saw and heard. They could not have wished to deceive. It is out of the question. As we read what is conveyed in the various histories, letters, and exhortations forming the apostolic literature, we are convinced that it is genuine and unimpeachable testimony to the awful and yet glorious facts on which our faith in the crucified and risen Saviour rests.

Thus each scriptural difficulty does not harass us as a life or death danger to our belief. It is a difficulty, not as to the truth of our creed, but as to the nature and degree of the guidance given to the writers who embody our creed. If the character of Christ is truly drawn, if His teaching is on the whole faithfully preserved, then we have His Life as our pattern, His Death as our Redemption, His Resurrection as the pledge of our immortality, even though we had to suppose that the witnesses were not gifted with infallibility. So our faith does not tremble in the balance with every puzzle in scriptural interpretation. The several hands that drew Christ's picture, the several witnesses that preserved His teaching, have made us know Him as He really was. They supplement each other. They balance each other ; their very variations in detail corroborate their general testimony.

But if the study of the canon makes us *cautious* as to the foundation of our faith, still more does it make us *sure* of it. It shows us the wonderful precautions taken to *keep* the witness, the love with which it was *cherished*, the care with which it was *sifted*, the determination with which all that was not reliable was *put aside*. Thus we are made sure of the genuineness of what was kept. If anything could show us the watchful guardianship of God's providence over His Church it is the phenomena presented by the growth of the canon. I dare say you are all familiar with the story of an Italian nobleman who, during the stern reign of Napoleon, underwent a long imprisonment. He had drunk deep of the cold rationalism of the eighteenth century, and went to prison an atheist. As he paced his little court he noticed one day a slight disturbance of its hard clay floor. Then in a few days a glistening point pushed itself up through the clay and mortar. As these rough impediments were got over, the hard sheath opened out, and a delicate plant shot up into the air. The prisoner watched from day to day with deep interest the growth of the little plant, the expanding of leaves that had been daintily folded in their protecting case, the issuing of a carefully covered bud, which opened out, petal after petal, into a lovely flower, with provision in its calyx for the infinite renewal of the plant's life. And through the teaching of this "lily of the field" the atheist left his prison a believer in his Father's wisdom and his Father's love. Have we not a similar lesson as we watch the growth and progress of the plant that has blossomed so beautifully and borne such precious fruit of world-teaching knowledge? Think of this "good thing coming out of Nazareth." Think of the circumstances through which it emerged— the rude, ignorant, and tumultuous people among whom its first readers and writers lived; the fierce prejudices, the fanatic hatred, the mingled scorn and persecution through which it had to push its way. Think of the difficulties of copying, preserving, and transmitting the fragmentary writings. Think of the enemies outside the Church, the rival parties within, the scantiness of knowledge everywhere. Think of how steadily, quietly this holy literature came into being as it was needed, pushed aside all entangling and misleading growths, extended its branches, opened out its blossoms, and shed forth its fragrance till the whole Church could feel its beauty and feed on its fruitage. Think of all this as you read the calm, beautiful verses of the New Testament, and then say if you can that there is there no sign of the presence and working of " a Power not ourselves that makes for righteousness."

With two thoughts I now draw this paper to its conclusion. (1) I have said, that for the foundation of our faith we rely, not on the inspiration, but on the *witness* of the New Testament writers. But in that very witness their inspiration is really implied. For they witness that Jesus was the Son of God, and that He commissioned and by His Holy Spirit guided certain apostles to carry His teaching into the world. And all the care and discrimination we saw exercised by the early Church about the canonical writings turned on one point—a matter of fact, not of opinion—their apostolicity. The spurious were rejected, the disputed were established, the acknowledged were cherished —all according to the one test, Were they

or were they not " genuine documents of the
apostolic age, containing the substance of the
apostolic testimony "?   Therefore, as we read
the New Testament, we can be sure that we
are reading what was taught by the apostles
of the Lord Jesus. We need not puzzle
ourselves as to theories of inspiration, as to
the exact way in which the Divine and
human elements were blended, as to how
far the celestial melody was affected by the
various voices which took it up and sang it.
We know all that we really want to know.
We know that, as we read our New Testament, we are sitting at the feet of the men
whom Jesus sent forth to teach in His name,
and to whom He promised that the Holy
Ghost would guide them into all truth.

(2) Once more, as we saw in our last lecture
that the best way to appreciate the planet's
glory is to look at its shining, so now we
may say, that to appreciate the beauty and
fragrance of this New Testament flower, the
best way is to look at it steadfastly and
breathe in its sweetness.   If the clearest

proof of Christianity is Christ, so the clearest proof of the inspiration of Scripture is Scripture itself. Its effect on the human heart and human conscience is a permanent miracle.

Read your New Testament with attention, with sympathy, with prayer. Read it sometimes rapidly, to catch its general spirit, sometimes thoughtfully, verse by verse, to appreciate the delicate shades of its meaning ; and as you find in it always something to meet the needs of your nature, probings to the depths of your conscience to convince you of sin, pictures of your Father and Saviour, promises of His pity and pardon to calm your fear, lofty ideals of life to stir you to exertion, strong motives to nerve you in battle against temptation, consolations to soothe you in sorrow, and promises that make all life bright as the beginning of heaven—as thus you study the canonical writings, you need hardly any other witness to convince you that "the gospel is the power of God unto salvation, to the Jew first, and also to the Gentile."

LECTURE III.

THE APOCRYPHAL GOSPELS.

By Rev. J. H. BERNARD, B.D.

LECTURE III.

THE APOCRYPHAL GOSPELS.

IT has been sometimes suggested by persons to whom the presence of the supernatural element in history is distasteful, that the books of the New Testament, and especially our four canonical Gospels, are but the product of that myth-making tendency which has frequently manifested itself among peoples of imperfect culture. Legends, we are told, always group themselves about any great personage after his life-work has been accomplished ; and it is in accordance with this law of the evolution of myth that our Gospels came to be written and received in the Christian community. There are many reasons which forbid us from accepting such a theory as an adequate account of the production of those sacred books, which are the most precious inheritance of Christendom ; I propose to point out here only one line of argument, which will, I believe, furnish a satisfactory answer to most minds. And it is this. It so happens that we are in possession of a number of books written in the early centuries with the intention of improving on the picture of our Lord's life drawn by the evangelists, and embodying a collection of legends which from time to time had grown up. These are generally called *The Apocryphal Gospels.* Here, then, we have samples of what the myth-making spirit of primitive Christianity actually accomplished ; if the canonical Gospels had grown up in the same way, we may be quite sure that there would be a marked similarity between the two classes of writings. If they were all produced under the same conditions, as the expression of the same pious interest, for the same object of the edification of the Christian Church, we should naturally expect that they would be of the same general character and

—within certain limits, inasmuch as they deal with the same subject — instinct with the same attractiveness and beauty. On the other hand, if we find (as I believe we shall find) that no words are strong enough to express the contrast which exists both in form and in spirit between the inspired writings of the evangelists and these miserable legends, we shall be forced to believe that the mythological capacities of the early centuries were not sufficient to produce the former, and that their origin must be traced to a higher source.

It may be well, in the first place, to remind ourselves what is implied in the phrase "apocryphal gospels." They are not to be confounded with the apocryphal books of the Old Testament that are often bound up with our Bibles ; these are described in our Sixth Article as, though not applicable to the establishment of doctrine, yet "read for example of life and instruction of manners," but no one is likely to make such a claim for the books of which we are now speaking. They are simply lives of our Lord which acquired a certain circulation in the early centuries, of uncertain authorship [1] and possessed of no official character. Irenæus tells us that in his day "an unspeakable number" of such books was known to exist. The causes which elicited them were very various. Some were written to gratify a pious curiosity; there was a desire to know something more of our Lord's life than is revealed in Holy Scripture, and so the demand created the supply. In these the popular legends of the locality would be naturally incorporated. Others were composed in the interest of different forms of heresy, which, finding no sufficient support in the words of Scripture, were fain to invent Scriptures for themselves. These latter have chiefly perished, and we only know them by repute and by a few fragments that are preserved in patristic literature ; any that have lived have apparently been polished and

---

[1] " Quarum occulta origo non claruit patribus."— Aug., *De Civ. Dei*, xv. 23.

pruned by successive editors of unimpeachable orthodoxy. Many of these "gospels"
are palpably forgeries, for they claim the
name of an author to which it is demon-
strable that they have no right; *e.g.*, the
Gospel of Nicodemus (in its present form
at least) was certainly not written by its
nominal author, nor could the *Gospel of
James* have been composed by either of the
apostles of that name. And yet these books
are not behindhand in putting forward their
authority to be heard ; both the Arabic *Gospel of the Infancy*[1] and the *Protevangel of
James*[2] laying express claim to inspiration.
Bishop Ellicott gives the following recipe for
making an apocryphal gospel. "To one part
of ancient traditions add five parts of pious
fraud and about as much of crude heresy ;
flavour with Docetism, Nestorianism, or
Eutychianism, according to taste ; mix in-

---

[1] At the beginning, "Auxiliante et favente summo
numine incipimus scribere librum miraculorum."

[2] In one MS. at end : "Θεὸν τὸν δόντά μοι τὴν δωρεὰν
καὶ τὴν σοφίαν τοῦ γράψαι τὴν ἱστορίαν ταύτην."

timately, and spread thinly on parchment." [1]
It must not then be forgotten that all these
books are admitted by every one to be
spurious and untrustworthy,—in many places
grotesque and irreverent; there is no question whatever as to their unhistorical character. It is just possible that grains of true
history may here and there be embedded in
masses of rubbish; but we are quite without
the means of distinguishing the true from the
false. For obvious reasons the quotations
here given will not by themselves give a fair
idea of the extreme puerility of these documents, for much would be too unpleasantly
grotesque to set down on paper.

The first thing that strikes us in looking
over the apocryphal gospels is that their
authors have chosen for their literary activity
periods as to which the canonical history is
silent. None of them gives an account of
our Lord's public ministry; the contrast with
the genuine Gospels would thus have been
rendered too striking. They may be roughly

[1] *Cambridge Essays* for 1856, p. 182.

divided into two classes—those which deal with our Lord's infancy and with the family history of the virgin mother ; and those which profess to give some account of our Lord's descent to Hades and the underworld after His crucifixion. Scripture being almost altogether silent on these subjects, the means of detecting the falsehood of the legends were not so available.

With reference to the first class, the most readable and interesting is called the *Protevangel of James*, probably by a Jew of that name. The points of contact between this and Justin Martyr seem to show that in some form—though not necessarily in its present form—it existed in the second century. It is the earliest repertory of ecclesiastical traditions respecting the Virgin Mary, and is not unlike a modern novel on sacred subjects. Somewhat longer and more fanciful, but derived from the same sources, is a gospel falsely attributed to St. Matthew, and with equal falsehood said to have been translated by St. Jerome from the Hebrew. And a still later, though somewhat more sober, recension of the same materials is the Latin *Gospel of the Nativity of Mary*, which was incorporated almost entire into the *Golden Legend* of the Middle Ages. The influence which these writings have exercised down to our own day is very considerable. The Roman Church, though condemning them as spurious, can yet point to no other source for certain legends which are incorporated in the Breviary. Thus, the traditional names of the parents of the Virgin Mary, Joachim and Anna, are venerated in the Roman Church still ; even nearer home we have traces of this mediæval belief. We have a St. Anne's Church in Dublin—no doubt, with an original, though perhaps unconscious, reference to the name preserved in the *Protevangel of James;* and the familiar collocation of Christian names, Mary Anne, is possibly to be traced to the same source. Again, there is here a long account of the presentation of the Virgin when a child in the Temple, an event which is still commemorated by the

Church of Rome. And, speaking generally, these three works are chiefly taken up with minute details tending to that glorification of the virgin mother which afterwards did so much to corrupt primitive Christianity.

It is interesting, however, to note how greatly these legends have influenced sacred art. A subject which has occupied several painters and which is best known from Perugino's famous picture is the Marriage of the Virgin. The story on which the pictures are founded is, that it being determined by the elders that Mary,—who had been dedicated to God by Anna,—should be betrothed to some pious man, perplexity arose as to the most appropriate suitor. Accordingly we read : " The angel of the Lord came to Zacharias and said, Go forth, and call together all the widowers among the people, and let every one of them bring his rod ; and he by whom the Lord shall show a sign shall be the husband of Mary. And the criers went out through all Judæa, and the trumpets of the Lord sounded, and all the people ran and met together. Joseph also, throwing away his axe, went out to meet them; and when they met together, they went to the high priest, taking every man his rod. After the high priest had received their rods he went into the Temple to pray; and when he had finished his prayer, he took the rods and went forth and distributed them, and there was no miracle attending them. The last rod was taken by Joseph, and, behold, a dove proceeded out of the rod and flew upon the head of Joseph,"[1] who was accordingly selected as the future guardian of the Virgin. We quote this story because it explains those pictorial representations of the Marriage of the Virgin, so common in mediæval art, in which Joseph is depicted as an old man with a green bough and a dove, and the disappointed suitors are represented as breaking their rods. The number of these pictures shows how enduring an impression this legend left on the mind of Christendom. The idea of the miraculous test mentioned

[1] *Protev. of James*, 8.

was no doubt borrowed from the budding of Aaron's rod.

Another illustration which is even more familiar may be derived from the *Gospel of the Pseudo-Matthew*, in which the scene of our Lord's Nativity is depicted as a cave, which became illuminated with a heavenly brightness by the presence of the Light of the world. On the third day after His birth, so the legend goes, the Holy Family removed themselves to a stable where an ox and an ass were sheltered—the animals in their adoration of the infant Saviour fulfilling the prophet's words : " The ox knoweth his owner, and the ass his master's crib " (Isa. i. 3).[1] Very fanciful and far-fetched, no doubt ; but mark how this idea, that an ox and an ass shared the same roof with our Lord, has come down through the centuries. It is constantly alluded to in mediæval sermons ; a well-known old Latin carol refers to it in the lines :

" Cognovit bos et asinus, quod puer erat Dominus."

---

[1] Reference is also made to the LXX. version of Hab. iii. 2.

There is hardly a picture, ancient or modern, of the scene of the Nativity which does not introduce these animals ; they are constantly represented on Christmas cards. And in a familiar little book which is still used for children, and which many of us doubtless read in extreme youth—*The Peep of Day*— the good authoress has given a wide currency to the legend. " There were," she says, "cows and asses in the stable," apparently not being conscious that she is quoting from a legend of the second century, and that her assertion has no scriptural authority.

In this *Gospel of the Pseudo-Matthew* much matter is added concerning the flight into Egypt, of a most extraordinary and incredible kind. For example, while the Holy Family are journeying they enter a cave which proves to be tenanted with dragons. The dragons do not injure them, but worship the Divine Child, thus fulfilling the injunction of the psalmist : " Praise the Lord from the earth, ye dragons, and all deeps " (Ps. cxlviii. 7). Lions and panthers do the same ; the lions being also used as beasts of burden. Then comes another episode celebrated in art, known as the *Bowing of the Palm*. A palm tree is made to bend to yield up its fruit, and to disclose a spring of water at its roots. As a reward, one of its branches is borne away by an angel to be planted in Paradise. The Holy Family next lodge in a temple in Egypt, where the idols fall in ruin to the ground; the governor of the country and the people are consequently led to believe in Christ. This last story is alluded to as authentic by Athanasius.[1]

But even these legends seem sober and plausible beside the stories which are told of our Lord's boyhood in this same document and in another "Gospel of the Infancy" which is attributed to St. Thomas the apostle, of which I have not yet spoken. This *Gospel of Thomas* is mentioned by Irenæus; and if the others from which have quoted deal chiefly with fictitious incidents in the life of the virgin mother, this

[1] *Oratio de Incarn. Verbi*, p. 62.

is full of miracles said to have been wrought by her Divine Son. Of their character we shall be able to judge in a moment ; but it appears plain that this account of them was composed with a distinct heretical bias ; the object of the original writer (who perhaps was a Gnostic of the second century) seems to have been to represent our Lord's manhood and growth in wisdom as quite unreal ; and His human nature and development are in consequence quite overshadowed by the superhuman majesty of His child-life. To take a few examples :

When the Lord was a child, it is said that He one Sabbath day made twelve sparrows out of clay, a number of other children being with Him. "When therefore one of the Jews had seen him doing this, he said to Joseph : Joseph, dost thou not see the child Jesus working on the Sabbath at what is not lawful for him to do? for He has made twelve sparrows of clay. And when Joseph heard this, he reproved him, saying : Wherefore dost thou on the Sabbath such things as are not lawful for us to do? And when Jesus heard Joseph, he struck his hands together and said to his sparrows, Fly! And at the voice of his command they began to fly. And in the sight and hearing of all that stood by he said to the birds: Go and fly through the earth and through all the world, and live. And when those that were there saw such miracles, they were filled with great astonishment."[1] This story penetrated even to Iceland. It has been found in a collection of Icelandic legends, where it is entitled, *The Saviour and the Golden Plovers.*[2]

Or again: "Now Jesus was six years old, and his mother sent him with a pitcher to the fountain to draw water with the children. And it came to pass after he had drawn the water that one of the children came against him and struck the pitcher and broke it. But Jesus stretched out the cloak which he had on, and took up in it as much water as

[1] *Pseudo-Matt.*, 27.
[2] See Cowper's *Apocryphal Gospels*, p. xxxii.

there had been in the pitcher, and carried it to his mother." [1]

Or again : " And his father was a carpenter, and at that time made ploughs and yokes. And a certain rich man ordered him to make him a couch. And one of the cross pieces being too short, they did not know what to do. Then the child Jesus said to his father Joseph, Put down the two pieces of wood, and make them even in the middle. And Joseph did as the child said to him. And Jesus stood at the other end, and took hold of the shorter piece of wood, and stretched it, and made it equal to the other. And his father Joseph saw it, and wondered, and embraced the child, and kissed him, saying, Blessed am I, because God has given me this child." [2]

Or lastly, not to multiply these idle tales : on two occasions the Divine Child is represented as using His superhuman power in the wantonness of cruelty for the purpose of

[1] *Pseudo-Matt.*, 33.
[2] *Thomas*, 13.

revenging Himself on His little playmates
for their offences against Him. "A boy, a
worker of iniquity," it is said, "ran up and
came against the shoulder of Jesus, wishing
to make sport of him, or to hurt him if he
could. And Jesus said to him : Thou shalt
not go back safe and sound from the way
that thou goest. And immediately he fell
down and died. And the parents of the
dead boy, who had seen what had happened,
cried out, saying, Where does this child come
from ?" and they complained to Joseph.
And after some delay the Lord restored the
boy again to life.[1]

Upon this characteristic of the apocryphal
gospels, that they are full of accounts of the
miracles of our Lord's infancy, a few words
should be said. In the first place, all such
legends seem directly to contradict St. John's
words in the second chapter of his gospel.
"This *beginning* of miracles did Jesus in
Cana of Galilee," writes the evangelist, in
reference to the miracle of the water that

[1] *Pseudo-Matt.*, 29.

was turned into wine at the wedding feast,
which implies (it has been plausibly argued)
that our Lord's boyhood had not been sig-
nalised by any such manifestations of His
superhuman origin as the apocryphal gospels
assign to Him.   And the general contrast
between the economy of miracle (if one may
so speak) apparent in the New Testament
and the prodigality of miracle in the legends
is very striking.   St. Mark notes (vi. 5), that
on one occasion in Galilee, our Lord "could
there do no mighty work, save that He laid
His hands upon a few sick folk, and healed
them"; but the writers of the apocryphal
gospels never regard any incident as satisfactorily told until it has been embellished
with marvel.   Even more important is it to
notice the contrast in the character of the
true and the false miracles.   Those of the
legends are mere vulgar wonders, like the
tricks of a thaumaturgist; they have no
moral significance, they convey no lesson.
The miracles of the New Testament are
really acted parables: they are not only

wonders, they are also *signs;* they are the
works of Him who displays His almighty
power most chiefly in showing mercy and
pity. But the alleged miracles of the infancy
are purposeless and wanton, even when they
are not deliberately cruel. There is an
absence of dignity about them, for they are
worked without any great or worthy object.
So then, even if we did not *know* that the
stories which have been cited are valueless
as history, being simply legends and myths
of which we can trace the development, we
should be led to suspect as much from the
character of what they have to tell. It has
often been pointed out, that in many features
the alleged patristic miracles were markedly
inferior to those of the New Testament.
Perhaps the most significant of these differences is this, that the true test of a genuine
miracle is a *moral* test; if the miracle sub-
serves not a worthy purpose, if it be unfruit-
ful in any good result, if the teaching by
which it is accompanied be not spiritually
elevating, then it stands self-condemned.

And that is precisely the case with the miracles attributed to our Lord in the Gospels of the Infancy. Other contrasts may here fitly be touched upon. The apocryphal gospels are entirely devoid of moral teaching, whether in the form of parable or otherwise. " Again, they hardly recognise the office of prophecy ; they make no reference to the struggles of the Church with the old forms of sin and evil reproduced from age to age till the final *regeneration of all things.* History in them becomes a mere collection of traditions, and is regarded neither as the fulfilment of the past nor as the type of the future." [1]

Many of these stories were eagerly assimilated by Mohammedanism. For example, we find in the Koran accounts of Mary being devoted to God by Anna, and of her being sustained during her sojourn in the Temple by divinely sent fruits ; of our Lord speaking while yet in His cradle, and of His manufacture of living sparrows out of mud.[2] These

[1] Westcott. *Introduction to Gospels*, p. 479.
[2] Sale's *Koran*, iii. 48, v. 119.

and similar legends probably reached Maho-
metans through the medium of a document
distinct from any of those yet cited, called
the *Arabic Gospel of the Infancy*, which is
said to be still in some repute among the
Nestorians of Syria. The date of its composition is uncertain, but it seems to be a
late compilation, probably as late as the fifth
century. It adds some touches which betray
its Eastern origin. It tells that the coming
of the wise men who were led by the star
to the infant Saviour was predicted by
Zoroaster, the Eastern sage ; and in addition to nearly all the prodigies recorded in
the earlier apocrypha, it has many peculiar
to itself, especially in connexion with the
flight into Egypt. During this journey many
miracles are recounted as having happened.
In one city a demoniac young woman is
healed, out of whom Satan departs in a form
possibly (as Bishop Ellicott remarks) only
too common—in the form of a young man.
On another occasion the travellers meet three
women journeying, and with them a mule

richly caparisoned, on which they bestow much affection. It appears on inquiry that the mule is their brother, who has been bewitched. When they hear of the prodigies which have accompanied the travels of the Holy Family they ask for help. "We beseech thee, therefore, they said, to have pity upon us. Then, grieving at their lot, the Lady Mary took up the Lord Jesus and put him on the mule's back ; and she wept as well as the women, and said to Jesus Christ : Alas! my son, heal this mule by thy mighty power, and make him a man endowed with reason as he was before. And when these words were uttered by the Lady Mary, his form was changed, and the mule became a young man free from every defect." [1]

The Eastern origin of this tale is apparent in every line ; it reminds us of the stories in the *Arabian Nights*, with which it is on a par in point of sobriety.

An anecdote not quite so grotesque follows close upon the last. "They come in

[1] Chap. 21.

their journey to a desert, and hearing that it
was infested by robbers, Joseph and Mary
resolve to cross this region by night. But as
they go along, behold, they see two robbers
lying in the way, and along with them a
great multitude of robbers who are their
associates, sleeping. Now these two robbers
into whose hands they have fallen are Titus
and Dumachus. Titus therefore says to
Dumachus : I beseech thee to let these
persons go freely, and so that our comrades
may not see them. And as Dumachus re-
fuses, Titus says to him again : Take to thy-
self forty drachmas from me, and hold this
as a pledge. At the same time he holds out
to him the belt which he had had about his
waist, to keep him from opening his mouth
or speaking. And the Lady Mary, seeing
that the robber had done them a kindness,
says to him : The Lord God will sustain
thee by His right hand, and will grant thee
remission of thy sins. And the Lord Jesus
answering says to his mother : Thirty years
hence, O my mother, the Jews will crucify

me at Jerusalem, and these two robbers will be raised upon the cross along with me, Titus on my right hand and Dumachus on my left ; and after that day Titus shall go before me into Paradise. And she said, God keep this from thee, my son. And they went thence towards a city of idols, which on their approach was changed into sandhills."[1] This and several other stories from the apocryphal gospels are familiar to English readers from being incorporated in Longfellow's *Golden Legend.* Another romance of equally good authority, however, represents the names of the two thieves as Dismas and Gestas.

We only add one more story from this Arabic collection of legends. Once upon a time in Bethlehem, it is said, the Divine Child with some others went into the shop of a dyer whose name was Salem. He was from home. They accordingly threw all the rags in the shop into a tub full of blue. When Salem returned he was much vexed, whereupon the Christ changed back each

[1] Chap. 23.

rag to its proper colour. So great a hold did this story take on the popular imagination that a dyer's shop, travellers say, is still in Persia called a Christ's shop.

Now it is not needful to occupy space in pointing out the fantastic character of these as spurious additions to the life of our Lord recorded in the canonical Gospels. They show at least two things : (1) the intense and overmastering curiosity which possessed men in early times to know something of the details of the Lord's childhood beyond the simple account given by St. Luke, that " He increased in wisdom and stature, and in favour with God and man " ; and they show (2) exactly what kind of Gospel the men of the first six centuries would have been able to construct by their own unaided efforts. Does any one want to know in what consists the inspiration of the Gospels ? As good a practical answer as need be given is to bid such a one read the apocryphal gospels. The difference between the two is like the difference between light and darkness. It has been noticed as "an astonishing proof of the Divine guidance vouchsafed to the evangelists, that no man of their time or since has been able to touch the picture of the Christ without debasing it." And the difficulty in speaking of the contrast is to use language which shall not appear exaggerated to those who are not familiar with the documents ; no language, we will be bold to say, could appear too strong to any one who has dispassionately read them for himself. For it must be remembered that here we have not selected by any means the most fanciful stories for quotation ; those only have been chosen which are suitable for our present purpose and which will bear quotation without exciting disgust. Many of the remainder are so irreverent and so foolish that the only effect of quotation would be to provoke a smile.

Let us now turn to the second and distinct class of this apocryphal literature, which professes to give an account of our Lord's trial before Pilate and His descent to the underworld. The most notable book in this series is called the *Gospel of Nicodemus*, or the *Acts of Pilate*. It was very popular in the Middle Ages, and upon it were based many of the details of the old mystery plays of the Passion. It was much read in England; indeed, almost simultaneously with the introduction of printing into Britain, it was published in black letter in 1509 by Wynkyn de Worde. It inspired the romance of the enchanter Merlin. And even in Ireland it had a great circulation. Prof. Atkinson has lately printed a translation of it taken from the Passions and Homilies of the Speckled Book, which is one of the treasures of the Royal Irish Academy. To understand the popularity of this work we must remember that there was a very early belief that Pontius Pilate became a convert to Christianity. In the calendar of the Ethiopic Church, he is canonized as a saint along with his wife Procla; and their festival is celebrated on June 25th. But, whether he was ever converted or not, it seems to be probable that some genuine report of Pilate to the Roman emperor, concerning the trial and crucifixion of our Lord, was extant in the second century, and that the book we now have is a debased and interpolated transcript of this. If such be the fact, there may be grains of true history enshrined in a good deal of later tradition. In any case, incidents such as the pleading of Nicodemus on behalf of our Lord, the charge of magic brought against the Christ, and the imprisonment of Joseph of Arimathæa for his partisanship were widely believed in the Middle Ages. The names of Dismas and Gestas for the two malefactors, of Procla for Pilate's wife, of Longinus for the soldier who pierced our Lord's side with a spear, of Veronica for the woman upon whose handkerchief the impression of the Lord's face was received (a story upon which Roman Catholics have enlarged), are all derived from this *Gospel of Nicodemus.* It is not of course suggested that these details are trustworthy ; but it is only fair

to point out that the *Gospel of Nicodemus*
is free from the follies which disfigure the
Gospels of the Infancy. It is in the main
an expansion for popular use of the narrative
contained in the closing chapters of St.
Matthew's Gospel. All the incidents are
told at greater length and with dramatic
additions. Thus, to quote from the recently
published Irish version : " Then said Pilate :
Well then, thou art a king ? Thou sayest
so anyhow, said the Lord ; and what thou
sayest is true, for I was born for that, and
for that I came into the world ; and every
one who is on the side of truth heareth me.
Pilate rejoined : The law saith that there
is no truth on earth. That is not so, said
Jesus ; truth will exist on earth so long as
I am in it." [1] Several incidents of this sort
are conceived with more good taste than we
should expect from our experience of the
other writings of this class ; but we come
back on the false and the fictitious when
we turn to the *Descent to the Underworld*,

[1] Atkinson. *Todd Lectures*, R.I.A., p. 363.

the last book it is necessary to mention. This is a manifest forgery, a pious fraud of the fifth century, written apparently to gratify the intruding curiosity of the vulgar as to the conditions of the world of spirit. It is also to be found in an Irish version in Prof. Atkinson's edition of the Passions and Homilies of the Speckled Book ; but our ancestors, in reading it, were occupying themselves, it is to be feared, with hopelessly unhistorical legends. The pith of this is a story told by Joseph of Arimathæa, who mentions that among those who arose from their graves in Jerusalem at our Lord's crucifixion were two men called Karinus and Leucius. We may pass over without further comment the fact that Leucius Karinus was the name of the well-known author of several heretical apocrypha. But leaving that aside, it is said that these two persons, being restored to life, and being questioned as to their experiences in Hades, wrote down separately for the elders of the synagogue the same verbatim account of what they heard and saw in the other world after death. They describe at great length a dispute, which took place between Satan and the Lord of Hades, as to the significance of a great light which illuminated even that gloomy region after the Passion of the Saviour. While they are considering what may mean these golden rays, which are in truth announcing the coming deliverance, suddenly they hear a voice of thunder saying : " Lift up your heads, O ye gates, and be ye lift up, ye iron doors, that the King of glory may come in." Our Lord then enters in the form of a man. Satan is vanquished, and the saints are signed with the cross and led forthwith into Paradise. Karinus and Leucius are allowed only three days to remain upon earth in order to write their narratives, which are found miraculously to correspond. "Immediately," says the legend, "they were changed into exceedingly white forms, and were seen no more. But what they had written was found to agree perfectly, the one not containing a single

9

letter more or less than the other. And Pilate wrote down all these transactions and placed the accounts in the public records."

When we have said that some of this is told dramatically and with reverence, we have said all that can charitably be urged for the stories of the *Descent to the Underworld.* People wanted to know exactly what was meant by the words in the creed, " He descended into hell"; and as materials for a true account were not at hand, nothing being recorded on the subject in Scripture, it is not surprising that the religious romance which was invented to supply the lack of revelation was not very edifying. It furnishes one more instance of the utter inability of the men of the early centuries to touch the narrative of the holy Gospels without spoiling it. The authors of this *Descent to Hades* were pious men,—of that there can be no doubt,—their piety is manifest on every page ; but not having clearly understood that a pious fraud is a contradiction in terms, that nothing is so pious

as the truth, their well-meant efforts to
add to the revelation of the risen Lord
only served to disfigure it. The *vulgarity*
of the Gospels of the Infancy is absent; but
credulity and *superstition* have become very
common by the time we reach this fifth
century romance.

Some will perhaps ask : Is there no possibility of any genuine words of our blessed
Lord being preserved in these legends ?
For if there were even such a possibility,
they would be worth reading for that
reason alone. To this question it must be
answered, that there is little hope of arriving
thus at any genuine words of the Lord.
Those which are attributed to Him in the
Gospels of the Infancy have not the ring of
genuineness which those have with which
we are familiar. They are unworthy of the
great Master, and we cannot believe them
to have proceeded from His lips. We say
nothing now, of course, of the possibility of
such precious fragments being preserved in
the patristic literature of the second and third

centuries. One or two sayings have come down to us which might perhaps have been spoken by the Christ, such as "Shew yourselves tried bankers," meaning, "Put your talents to good use," preserved by Origen; or, "In whatsoever I may find you, in this also will I judge you," preserved by Justin Martyr; or again, "He who is near Me is near the fire": but there are certainly none such recorded in the apocryphal gospels, which are untrustworthy from first to last. Yet these wild legends have many uses other than those which they supply in an evidential point of view from their absolute contrast to the inspired writings of the evangelists. This is what we have especially endeavoured to draw out in this paper; but they have many other lessons for the men and women of our generation. It is always instructive to look at any subject of interest to ourselves from a standpoint which is not our own; and from the wide circulation and popularity of these documents in the Middle Ages we get a very fair idea of the tastes of mediæval Christianity. The Christian public of the Middle Ages were very credulous and superstitious. Granted ; but they were possessed with an overwhelming certainty of the majesty of the Person of our Lord Jesus Christ. Nothing was too great, nothing too marvellous to be attributed to Him. And so far they were unquestionably right. We have got beyond them (as the world has grown wiser) in our appreciation of evidence, in our respect for truth, in our quickened moral sensitiveness as to what is and what is not worthy of Almighty God ; and hence we are saved from the fetters of superstition which tied and bound many of them. All this is true : but yet, if, in freeing ourselves from superstition, we have grown incredulous of miracle as such ; if, in limiting the demands upon faith, we have exalted too much the province of reason ; if, in vindicating the claims of man's intellect, we have learnt to forget the essentially supernatural character of Christianity,—then we are in worse case than they. We hear a great deal of the dangers of superstition, and truly they are manifold ; but it is worth seriously considering whether there is really so serious a danger in this direction as in that other of absolute infidelity. As Bacon tells us,[1] "There is a superstition in avoiding superstition ; when men think to do best, if they go furthest from the superstition commonly received : therefore, care should be had that (as it fareth in ill purgings), the good be not taken away with the bad ; which commonly is done, when the people is the reformer." It is a very easy thing for a writer to point out the extravagances of the apocryphal gospels, it is easy for the reader to acquiesce ; it is not so easy to insure that, while we see the mote in our brother's eye, we shall also see the beam in our own. There is a prevalent tendency to minimize as far as may be the supernatural element in Christianity, a tendency which is really most pernicious. For if Christianity is true, it is rooted and

[1] Essay xvii. *Of Superstition.*

grounded in supernaturalism. And so let us not forget that the reason we reject the stories of the early forgers, of which an account has been given, is that we can prove them to be forgeries ; we know all about their origin and growth. They are the myths of primitive Christianity, and in this stand in sharp contradistinction to its history. We do *not* reject them because of their miraculous character as such ; we reject them because the miracles are not morally beneficial, because they are purposeless, and because they are badly attested. The romances which relate them are not authentic, they have no real connexion with the persons whose names they bear. But yet, though rejecting, and thankfully rejecting, the superstitions of mediævalism, it is not well to forget that it is from the faith of mediæval Christianity that we inherit our own. We are far beyond the authors of the Arabic Gospel or the first readers of the Speckled Book in science and in sobriety of judgment ; but nevertheless we hold substantially the same faith—a faith which led them, in spite of its imperfection, to look beyond the surface of things to that kingdom where (say the old Irish homilists) there is life without death, youth without age, joy without sorrow, peace without strife, unity without division, and great gladness without end for evermore.

LECTURE IV.

THE MIRACULOUS IN EARLY CHRISTIAN LITERATURE.

BY REV. J. H. BERNARD, B.D.

LECTURE IV.

THE MIRACULOUS IN EARLY CHRISTIAN LITERATURE.

ONE of the commonest objections urged at the present day against our belief in the miraculous character of Christianity appeals to a tendency in human nature which is very strong in most people; namely, the tendency to hasty generalization. Thus, we are told that, if we accept as true the record of our Lord's miracles, and especially the miracle of His Resurrection, we should, in order to be consistent, pledge ourselves also to belief in numberless other alleged occurrences which seem miraculous or out of the ordinary course of nature. On the other hand, if we reject the so called wonders of paganism and the miracles of the Church of

Rome, it is supposed that we have no better ground for believing in the supernatural origin of Christianity, and that therefore this also should be given up as impossible to be held by an enlightened rationalism. And in particular it has been urged that the Gospel miracles form only the beginning of a recorded series of wonders which have lasted down to the present day; that ecclesiastical history from the days of the apostles to our own teems with miracles, many of them well attested by apparently good witnesses; and that, as our historical vision takes a wider range, we shall see the necessity of either rejecting all or accepting all alike.

Now, it is not needful to spend time in showing the illogical character of this reasoning. If there is one principle clearer than another as to evidence, it is this, that every case which comes under review must be judged on its own merits, no two sets of witnesses being exactly alike. It has been argued with some plausibility that in the miracles recorded throughout the whole Bible

we can trace a consistent plan in their dis-
tribution and occurrence. Thus Archbishop
Trench has noticed that the miracles of the
Old Testament are chiefly grouped round
two great epochs in the history of the theo-
cratic kingdom—that of its foundation under
Moses and Joshua, and that of its restoration
by Elijah and Elisha; and the miracles of
the New Testament also ushered in a new
era for the whole world. And it has been
said that no such *crisis* having since occurred,
there is no antecedent probability in favour
of miracles having happened since. But this
is mere speculation: we shall confine ourselves strictly to the evidence; for what the
objection rests upon is the plea that the
evidence for mediæval miracles is just as
good as for those of the Bible. Now, if it
could be shown that all the miracles of
ecclesiastical history were of the same general
type, of the same antecedent probability, and
attested by as remarkable and tried evidence
as the miracles of the New Testament, then
the objection might be applicable; but as

this cannot be shown, it must not be assumed without a protest.

It is here proposed to consider briefly the testimony to contemporary miracles which we find in early Christian literature, and I believe we shall see that the facts do not at all warrant the conclusion to which I have alluded as supposed to be binding on reasonable men. It is not plain that the miraculous of ecclesiastical history stands on the same level, whether in regard to quality or in regard to evidence, as the miraculous of the New Testament.

But this having been said, a protest should be entered against the assumption, that because a fact is not sufficiently attested, therefore it cannot be true. There is another alternative besides true or false, namely " not proven "; and this we shall have to bear in mind if we wish to avoid over-statement of our case. And so it is not here asserted, nor is it even implied, that miracles could not or even did not happen after apostolic times ; it will be time enough to draw our inferences when the facts are before us. There have been many different opinions held regarding the cessation of the miraculous gifts entrusted to the apostolic Church. The Church of Rome believes that they are still in her possession. Many Protestants, on the other hand, believe that they died with the apostolic company. The chief reason alleged for this latter opinion is apparently based on the assumption that miracles are only given for evidential purposes, that their sole function is to certify the Divine character of revelation, and that when this has been sufficiently established, their work is done, and they may not be expected to continue. And, curiously enough, but most unreasonably, it has been assumed that the apostles could not have worked any miracle save those recorded in Scripture, or at least that no trustworthy record could be preserved of such. Between these extreme views are to be ranked the great body of old English divines, *e.g.*, Dodwell and Tillotson, who held that miracles were occasional in the Christian Church until the time of Constantine, at the beginning of the fourth century, when, Christianity being established by the civil power, it no longer needed such supernatural assistance. Thus Fuller explains that "miracles are the swaddling clothes of the infant Churches." And yet another view has commended itself to many, as most in accordance with the evidence we possess; namely that, as Bishop Kaye[1] puts it, "the power of working miracles extended to, but not beyond, the disciples upon whom the apostles conferred it by imposition of their hands." Let us first see what Scripture tells us. We have recorded in Mark xvi. 17 a remarkable promise given by our Lord to His apostles : "These signs shall follow them that believe : In My name shall they cast out devils ; they shall speak with new tongues ; they shall take up serpents; and if they drink any deadly thing, it shall not hurt them; they shall lay hands on the sick, and they shall recover." And if we turn to the Acts of the Apostles we shall find instances of all these

[1] *Tertullian*, p. 49.

powers (with the exception of immunity from poison) being enjoyed, not only by the original eleven and by St. Paul, but by many other disciples. (i.) Thus the gift of tongues found its fulfilment at Pentecost, and is alluded to by St. Paul in his epistles. Prophecy, which was akin to this, is frequently spoken of as a " sign " of an apostle. Agabus (Acts xi. 28) not only predicted a famine, but also warned St. Paul of what would happen to him at Jerusalem (Acts xxi. 10). Twelve un-named Ephesian disciples on whom St. Paul laid his hands were endued with this gift (Acts xix. 6), as were also the four daughters of St. Philip the Evangelist (Acts xxi. 9). (ii.) Again the story of St. Paul and the viper at Malta (Acts xxviii. 3) furnishes an exemplification of the words "they shall take up serpents." (iii.) The mysterious power of exorcism, or the casting out of devils, was exercised by St. Paul in the case of the young woman at Philippi "who brought her masters much gain by soothsaying " (Acts xvi. 16). (iv.) And the gift of healing was used by St.

Paul for the relief of Publius at Malta (Acts xxviii. 8), by St. Peter for the cure of the palsied Æneas at Lydda (Acts ix. 33), and is even said to have displayed itself through the medium of St. Peter's shadow (Acts v. 15) and St. Paul's clothing (Acts xix. 12), " insomuch that unto the sick were carried away from his body handkerchiefs or aprons, and the diseases departed from them, and the evil spirits went out." The restoration of Eutychus (Acts xx. 9) and of Dorcas (Acts ix. 36) will be in our remembrance. And the general expression, "signs and wonders" is used of the doings of St. Paul and St. Barnabas at Iconium (Acts xiv. 3), of St. Stephen at Jerusalem (Acts vi. 8), and of St. Philip the Evangelist at Samaria (Acts viii. 6).

We see, therefore, that these Divine gifts, promised by our Lord to His Church, were at least occasionally exercised by individuals a quarter of a century after His Ascension, and that they were not confined to the apostolic company, but shared in by numerous persons. Hence I think we should not be surprised if

we found in the early literature of the second
century records of many miracles such as the
above. Many persons must have been living
in the time of Clement and Polycarp who
had themselves received a measure of miraculous power at the hands of the apostles.
And yet we find in the literature of the
earliest sub-apostolic age few and scanty
references of this character. Our records of
this period are fragmentary and imperfect, it
is true ; but yet it is remarkable that they
tell us so little on the subject. With a few
notable exceptions, of which something shall
be said farther on, there is no trace up to the
end of the second century of any miraculous
gift still existing in the primitive Church,
save those of *prophecy* and *healing*, including *exorcism*, both of which are frequently
mentioned.

And first as to *prophecy*. In the *Shepherd
of Hermas* (Command xi.) rules are laid
down for the discernment of false prophets ;
thus quite early in the second century is
implied the continued presence of the pro-

phetic power. Similarly, in the manual known as the *Didache* or "Teaching of the Twelve Apostles," the abuse of the "grace of prophecy" is seriously reckoned with. A little later Justin Martyr (Dial. 308 B.) says, "With us even up to the present time are continued the prophetic gifts of the Spirit."[1] Upon these notices two remarks may be offered. In the first place it is obvious that of all Divine gifts "prophecy" of this sort is that which would most easily lend itself to imposture ; and we observe that the earliest notice of the power implies also the presence of its counterfeit. And further Justin is apparently surprised that the gift should have lasted to his day, for he says, "*even* up to the present" ; from which we may gather, as it seems, that instances of genuine prophecy in his day and in his neighbourhood were not very numerous.

The gift of *healing* is also spoken of as present in the Church of the second

[1] παρὰ γὰρ ἡμῖν καὶ μέχρι νῦν προφητικὰ χαρίσματά ἐστιν. Cf. *Dial.* 315 B.

century. It is specified by Justin Martyr,[1] though he does not give any particular instance in which it had proved beneficial within his knowledge, an omission which considerably detracts from the value of his testimony. Origen [2] also asserts that " many give proofs to those who have been healed through their power that they have attained a miraculous power through this faith ; while over those who require healing they invoke no other power than the Almighty God and Jesus Christ, together with the preaching of His Gospel. Therefore have I seen many persons rescued from severe circumstances of delirium and fancy, and many other evils which no man and none of your demons could cure."

But the commonest exemplification of this gift was displayed in the driving out of devils ; exorcism is regarded quite as a thing of course by the second century Fathers. Justin Martyr builds up an argument upon

[1] *Dial.* 258 A.

[2] *Contra Celsum*, iii. 24.

it.[1] "That Jesus was made man for the sake of the believers and for the subversion of demons is manifest from what is done before your eyes all over the world ; when those who are vexed by demons whom your own enchanters could not cure, are healed by our Christians abjuring and casting out the demons in the name of Jesus." And the fervid and passionate Tertullian gives this bold challenge to his heathen opponents :[2] "Bring before your tribunals a man possessed with a demon ; the evil spirit, if commanded by a Christian, will speak and confess himself a demon." These passages, strong as they are, are however not convincing that any miracle was here worked. We may notice the extravagance of the claim made by Origen and Tertullian : that power which in the days of the apostles

[1] Apol. 45, A. Cf. also *Dial.* 247 C, 302 A, 311 B, 350 B, 361 C.

[2] Apol. 23. Cf. also Apol. 37, 43 ; *De Spectac.* 29 ; *De Test. An.* 3 ; *Ad Scap.* 2 ; *De Corona,* 11 ; *De Idolol.* 11 ; in which passages allusion is made to the expulsion of demons as a common occurrence.

was confined to them and those on whom they had laid their hands—which again was only within their power on special occasions when they were moved by a special Divine impulse—is here alleged to be the common property of all Christian people, and to be susceptible of exercise at any moment and on any occasion. Again, we must remember that phenomena of this sort are often quite explicable without any recourse to supernatural agency ; the power of a strong will over a weak one would sufficiently account for everything described by Tertullian. But all the Fathers of this period believed in the reality of magic, and so, perhaps, saw the miraculous in very ordinary events. We must not be too ready to despise them for this. It is not so long since the inhabitants of these islands believed in witchcraft, and attempted to put down witches by attaching the extreme penalty of the law to their supposed crimes. Witches were believed in by so intelligent a man and sagacious a judge as Sir Matthew Hale, by so able a physician as

Sir Thomas Browne, the author of *Religio Medici*.[1] And in later times John Wesley said,[2] "The giving up of witchcraft is the giving up the Bible," and confidently affirmed that "the course which he and his coadjutors had taken was approved by miracles" of healing.[3] But there is another circumstance about this second century belief in magic to which your attention should be called. The people who held it most strongly yet admitted a broad interval between the wonders of the thaumaturgists, whether pagan or Christian, and the genuine miraculous. So, too, you remember, the Jews of our Lord's time practised thaumaturgy of a kind ; but yet they plainly thought there was some tremendous difference between their own feats and His wonderful works ; else why did they refuse to give credence to these latter ?[4]

---

[1] See Goodwin, *Foundations of Creed*, p. 372.

[2] See Farrar, *History of Interpretation*, p. 40.

[3] See Southey's *Life of Wesley*, vol. i., p. 277 ; vol. ii., pp. 153, 199.

[4] Cf. Mozley, *Bampton Lectures*, pp. 164, 297.

Thus, when the heathen critics of early times were confronted with the assertion of our Lord's Resurrection, they answered at once that it was impossible that a dead man should come to life again, although they had their own magical arts going on. To take a specific example, Pliny the Elder was a believer in natural magic ; but he said distinctly that to raise a person from the dead was beyond the power of the gods to accomplish.[1] And in like manner Origen remarks of the pagans, " The mystery of the Resurrection is spoken of by the unbelieving with ridicule." [2] Now many of the Fathers draw just such a distinction between the "miracles" of their own and of the apostolic age, placing the latter on a pinnacle by themselves. For example, when we go on to the fourth century, we find Chrysostom saying that "all the men of his time together"[3] could not do as much as St. Paul's handker-

[1] *Nat. Hist.* ii. 5, 7.
[2] *Contra Celsum,* 1, 7.
[3] οἱ δὲ νῦν πάντες ὁμοῦ.   *De Sacerdo'.* iv. 3, fin.

chiefs; and he implies that in his day there were no raisings from the dead.[1] And Augustine explains that miracles, being especially signal events, and meant to awaken men from the torpor of custom, are not to be expected in every age[2]—a sensible remark, which, however, did not keep him, as we shall see, from over-credulity. It is then plain, that the admitted difference in kind between the miracles of Christ and the alleged miracles of subsequent centuries makes us feel somewhat dubious as to whether these latter were genuine miracles at all.[3] Further, as early as Tertullian, we

[1] Cf. also Hom. in 1 Cor. vi. 2, 3 : "Argue not, because miracles do not happen now, that they did not happen then. . . . In those times they were profitable, and now they are not."

[2] *De Lazar.* iv. 3 : "If God saw that the raising of the dead would profit the living, He would not have omitted it." (Quoted by Newman, *On Miracles*, p. 140.)

[3] *De Util. Credendi*, 16 : "Cur (inquis) ista modo non fiunt ? Quia non moverent nisi mira essent ; et si solita essentia mira non essent." Cf. also *De Civ. Dei*, xxii. 8, 1 : "Nam etiam nunc fiunt miracula in

get a distinct intimation that the miraculous powers which had been exerted by the apostles no longer existed [1]—for after saying that the apostles had spiritual powers peculiar to themselves Tertullian adds : " For they raised the dead, which God alone can do ; and they healed the sick, which none but Christ did." If such occurrences were even occasional in his day, this language would be strange. Of the gradual cessation of the miraculous, Origen thus speaks : " Miracles began with the preaching of Jesus, were multiplied after His ascension, and then again decreased ; but even now some traces of them remain with a few, whose souls are

ejus nomine, sive per sacramenta ejus, sive per orationes vel memorias sanctorum ejus ; sed non eadem claritate illustrantur, ut tanta quanta illa gloria diffamentur" ; and " Cur, inquiunt, nunc illa miracula, quæ prædicatis facta esse, non fiunt ? Possem quidem dicere, necessaria fuisse, priusquam crederet mundus, ad hoc ut crederet mundus" (*ib.*).

[1] *De Pud. c.* 21. " Nam et [*sc.* apostoli] mortuos suscitaverunt quod Deus solus ; et debiles redinte graverunt, quod nemo nisi Christus."

cleansed by the word." [1]   We find then (i.)
that by the end of the second century and
beginning of the third century there is a
growing suspicion that miracles are dying
out.   (ii.) We find that such miracles as are
recorded as late as this are generally
regarded as different in kind from those of
the apostolic age; and (iii.) in the earliest
age of post-apostolic Christianity, the "miracles" we read of are almost without exception those of prophecy, healing, and exorcism.
But exceptions there are, so interesting that
they require separate treatment.

Eusebius the historian [2] has preserved for
us fragments of the writings of one Papias,
who was bishop of Hierapolis in the second
century, an associate of Polycarp, and probably a disciple of St. John; and among
other particulars he notes " certain wonderful
accounts" that they contain.   " For," says
Eusebius, "that the Apostle Philip abode
at Hierapolis with his daughters, has been

---

[1] *Contra Celsum*, i. 2.   [2] *H. E.* iii. 39, 9.

stated above; but we must now show how Papias, coming to them, received a marvellous account from the daughters of Philip: for he relates that in his time a resurrection of a dead person took place. Another wonderful event happened respecting Justus, surnamed Barsabas, who, though he drank a deadly poison, received no hurt through the grace of the Lord. This Justus is the one who was elected into the place of Judas the traitor by the holy apostles after the Ascension of the Saviour, as is recorded in the book of the Acts." It was remarked a few pages back, that we find in the Acts no instance of the fulfilment of the Lord's promise to His apostles, "if they drink any deadly thing, it shall not hurt them," though we have abundant illustration of the outpouring of the other gifts enumerated in Mark xvi. 17. So it is interesting to find a tradition put in writing by one who was a disciple of St. John and a prominent person in the earliest sub-apostolic age, that Justus Barsabas escaped the fatal effects of poison " through the grace of the Lord." No doubt the story may not be true ; Papias may have been deceived in the matter—he only professes to have got the account from hearsay ; but yet there is nothing inherently unlikely in what he states to any one who believes in the supernatural origin of Christianity. But the first part of the extract from Papias is even more remarkable : "that in his time a resurrection of a dead person took place." As has been already noted, Papias does not give this on his own authority; it was told to him by the daughters of St. Philip the Evangelist, who had settled at Hierapolis, of which place Papias was bishop. Of these persons we read in Acts viii. and xxi., St. Philip being accredited by "signs and wonders," and his daughters being described as endowed with the gift of prophecy. And it is quite possible that they may have been eyewitnesses of some such event as the raising of Dorcas by St. Peter, which Papias, having heard of it from eyewitnesses, might perhaps describe as having happened in his day. But it is hardly worth

while to go into possibilities of this sort ; a
more interesting thing is to notice, that Papias
virtually implies that he himself never saw
any such occurrence, his only knowledge of
" miracle " of this kind being derived from
hearsay ; he does not even mention the name
of the person who was thus raised from the
dead. So that, instead of concluding from this
notice, even supposing that it enshrines a true
tradition, that miracles were frequent in the
time of Papias, an exactly opposite inference
is to be drawn. If they were frequent, if he
had ever seen one himself, he would have told
us of it ; or, to speak more accurately, Eusebius would not have selected for quotation a
second-hand story, if the direct evidence of
an eyewitness were on record.

We now proceed to quote the most striking
account of " miracles " to be found in the
Christian literature of the second century.
Irenæus, a disciple of Polycarp, was bishop of
Lyons at the end of that century. He wrote
a controversial treatise against the heretics of
his day, which has come down to us. In the

course of his argument, when speaking of the
followers of one Simon, a heretic, and their
inability to work miracles, he proceeds : [1]
" They can neither give sight to the blind,
nor hearing to the deaf, nor put to flight all
demons, except those which are sent into
others by themselves, if they can indeed even
do this. Nor can they cure the weak, or the
lame, or the paralytic, or those who are
troubled in any other part of the body, as
often happens to be done in respect of bodily
infirmity. Nor can they furnish effective
remedies for those external accidents which
may occur. And so far are they from raising
the dead, as the Lord raised them, and the
apostles did by means of prayer, and as
when frequently in the brotherhood the whole
Church in the locality, having made petition
with much fasting and prayer, the spirit of
the dead one has returned, and the man has
been given back to the prayers of the saints
— (so far are they from doing this) that they
do not believe that it can possibly be done,

[1] *Adv. Hær.* II. xxxi. § 2.

and they think that resurrection from the dead merely means a recognition of the truth of their tenets." . . . But on the other hand, as Irenæus insists in the next chapter, "those who are in truth (the Lord's) disciples, having received grace from Him, do in His name perform (miracles) for the benefit of other men, according to the gift which each one has received from Him. For some certainly and truly drive out demons, so that those who have been cleansed from the evil spirits frequently believe and are in the Church. Others have foreknowledge of things to come, and visions, and prophetic sayings. Others heal the sick by imposition of their hands, and they are restored to health. Yea, more-over, as we said, even the dead were raised, and abode with us many years.[1] What more shall I say? It is not possible to tell the number of the gifts which the Church throughout all the world has received from God in the name of Jesus Christ, who was crucified under Pontius Pilate, and which she

[1] ἠγέρθησαν καὶ παρέμειναν σὺν ἡμῖν ἱκανοῖς ἔτεσι.

exerts day by day for the welfare of the nations, neither deceiving any nor taking any reward for such. For as freely as she hath received from God, so freely doth she minister." [1]

The date of this treatise is about 185 A.D., and it is to be observed that the miracles put prominently forward by Irenæus in his argument, as affording a criterion of the truth of the doctrine of the Church, are, as usual, *prophecy*, *healing*, and *exorcism*. These he speaks of much in the way in which we have seen that Justin Martyr and Tertullian do; and it is not necessary to add anything to what has been said about their evidence, further than this : Irenæus is here writing in the heat of controversy ; his language is passionate and rhetorical, and he deals altogether in general statements; he has not produced a single specific instance. There is a want of particularity and detail about what he says, which seriously detracts from the value of his testimony. Nevertheless, however, many

[1] Cf. also *Adv. Hær.* V. vi. § 1, for a similar claim.

writers, *e.g.*, the cautious and learned Hooker,[1] have supposed that there were still in the time of Irenæus traces of that supernatural power which was manifested in the apostolic and sub-apostolic Church, and that we have here a reference which, though perhaps exaggerated, yet embodies historic facts. But it will be asked, Is this meant to apply to what Irenæus says about the raising of dead persons, as well as to his remarks about the prevalence of prophecy and the power of exorcism ? Well, Hooker accepted the whole statement as true without question and without qualification, and so have others since his time. But it may be argued with considerable justice, that what Irenæus tells us about gifts of healing, etc., seems to stand on a quite different level from what he says about the bringing of the dead to life. For in the passages cited above there is a sudden and unexpected change of tense when he begins to speak of this greatest of miracles. Healing, exorcism, and prophecy—these, he

[1] *E. P.* v. lxvi. 3.

asserts, are matters of present experience, but he never says that about resurrections from the dead. " It often happened," *i.e.* in the past ; " they were raised up," *i e.* again at some time now gone by. The use of the past tense here and here alone implies, we may say, that Irenæus had not witnessed an example with his own eyes, or, at least, that such occurrences were not usual when he was writing. And so when he states, " Even the dead were raised and abode with us many years," it does not appear that he means anything more than this—that such events happened within living memory. Now Irenæus was a disciple of Polycarp, and Polycarp was a disciple of St. John ; so that if we view his statement thus, it will not appear so extraordinary. But the inference from the whole passage is, we believe, that these major miracles no longer happened—an inference which is corroborated by all the testimony we have got. For example, we read elsewhere that a Greek of high birth, by name Autolycus, promised Theophilus, who was

bishop of Antioch about the time of Irenæus
that if he could be gratified with the sight of
a single person who had been actually raised
from the dead, he would immediately believe
in a resurrection after death. But the challenge was declined, Theophilus remarking
that there would be no moral value in a
faith thus persuaded, as there is nothing
meritorious in believing what we actually
see. However, the good bishop does not
state that he knows of a single specific instance ; and it is hardly likely that, if he
had known of any such, he would not have
produced it for the purpose of convincing his
noble opponent.[1]

But if the "gifts" of the Church seem
to have grown scarcer and scarcer as the
second century went on, it is also to be
noticed that miracles of the most astounding
character abound in the records of ecclesi-

[1] It has been often remarked that this want of detail
is a general characteristic of the testimony of the
period. See Newman, *Essay on Miracles*, p. 130, and
Mozley, *Bampton Lectures*, p. 295.

astical history from the times of the Council of Nice onward. And it may be fairly enough demanded of us to give some reason why we do not accept the latter as true. It would be impossible to deal completely with so large a subject in the short space which remains, but we shall mention a few considerations as to the character of many alleged miracles, and as to the quality of the evidence by which they are attested, which give us reasonable grounds for denying that they are at all comparable to those of the apostolic age. It must ever be remembered that there are miracles — and miracles.

(1) There are a great number of recorded events, seemingly miraculous, which on examination can be resolved into false perceptions, or deceptions of sense ; these are for the most part cases of visions or voices.[1] To take a modern instance, the vision of Colonel Gardiner has been often spoken of as miraculous. Now we here cite Dr. Dod-

[1] See Paley's *Evidences.* Part II., chap. i.

dridge's account of it,[1] that the reader may judge for himself. Colonel Gardiner, who was a man of profligate life, was whiling away an hour one evening reading when suddenly "he saw an unusual blaze of light fall on the book, . . . which he at first imagined might happen by some accident in the candle. But lifting up his eyes, he apprehended, to his extreme amazement, that there was before him, as it were suspended in the air, a visible representation of our Lord upon the cross, surrounded on all sides with a glory ; and was impressed as if a voice, or something equivalent to a voice, had come to him to this effect, for he was not confident as to the very words, ' O sinner, did I suffer this for thee ? and are these the returns ? ' But whether this were an audible voice, or only a strong impression on his mind equally striking, he did not seem very confident ; though, to the best of my remembrance, he rather judged it to be the former." This will serve well as a type of a very large

[1] *Works*, vol. i., p. 248.

number of so called ecclesiastical miracles (such as the vision of the cross in the heavens which Constantine saw) ; they are almost all given on the authority of a solitary witness, depending on the evidence of one sense. They are only momentary visions ; the sensible proof of their reality is gone once the vision is over. And besides the risk of delusion which attaches to these, there is the risk also of imposture. The account cannot be examined at the moment, and in a time of hurry and confusion it may not be difficult for men of influence to gain credit for any story which they may wish to have believed.

(2) Again, it often happens that in the accounts of many alleged miracles there is nothing in the story which infallibly proves the presence of supernatural agency. For example, we have an ancient record of the martyrdom of Polycarp, which took place about 155 A.D. In this we read as follows : " The fire making the appearance of a vault, like the sail of a vessel filled by the wind,

made a wall round about the body of the
martyr ; and it was then in the midst not
like flesh burning, but like gold and silver
refined in a furnace. For we perceived such
a fragrant smell as if it were the wafted
odour of frankincense or some other precious
stone. Whereupon one of the executioners
to hasten his death stabbed him with a
sword, and his blood from the wound put
out the fire." Now similar phenomena have
been recorded as happening on other occasions, *e.g.* at the martyrdoms of Savona-
rola and Hooper ;[1] and it is obvious that
they can be readily enough explained as the
operations of natural forces, a little exaggerated perhaps by pious enthusiasm. Very
many so called miracles of all ages are of
this low level ; they do not properly rise
into the region of the supernatural at all.
Another famous second century illustration is
found in the story of the Thundering Legion,
which Eusebius thus describes :[2] "It is said

---

[1] See Lightfoot. *Apostolic Fathers*, II. i. 599.
[2] Eus., *H. E.* v. 5 ; cf. v. 1. § 35.

that when Marcus Aurelius Cæsar was forming his troops in order of battle against the
Germans and Sarmatians, he was reduced to
extremities by a failure of water. Meanwhile
the soldiers in the so called Melitene legion,
which for its faith remains to this day, knelt
down upon the ground, as we are accustomed
to do in prayer, and betook themselves to
supplication. And whereas this sight was
strange to the enemy, another still more
strange happened immediately — thunder-
bolts which caused the enemy's flight and
overthrow ; and upon the army to which the
men were attached who had called upon
God, a rain which restored it entirely when
it was all but perishing by thirst." Now
that during the German war the Roman
army suffered severely from want of water,
and was relieved from a situation of great
peril by a seasonable shower of rain, which
had previously been prayed for by the
Christians in the army, may be quite
true. It is a story for which there is
heathen as well as Christian authority ; but

it need not have been a miracle—in any other sense than that in which every answer to prayer is a miracle. We may take a third instance illustrating this tendency to observe miracle where really there was none —a tendency due to an intense belief in the overruling providence of God, coupled with grave ignorance as to the laws of nature and the operations of natural forces. In the account which Eusebius gives of the martyrs of Palestine during the Diocletian persecution, he notes that horrible barbarities were practised at Cæsarea, and thereupon he makes the following innocent comment.[1] These atrocities having gone on for many days "a strange thing happened. The air happened to be clear and bright, and the aspect of the sky most serene. Then suddenly from the greater part of the columns that supported the public porticoes issued drops like tears, and the market places and streets, though there was no moisture in the air, I know not whence it came, were sprinkled

[1] *De Mart. Pal.* ix. 12.

with water, and became wet ; so that it was immediately spread abroad among all, that in an unaccountable manner the earth wept, not being able to endure the extreme impiety of these deeds ; and to address a reproof to men of a relentless and callous nature the very stones and senseless matter could bewail these facts. I well know that this account may appear, perhaps, an idle tale and fable to posterity, but it was not so to those who had its truth confirmed by their presence at the time." Here, again, a perfectly natural occurrence—apparently some unusual sweating of the colonnades—is exaggerated by the pious historian into a testimony to the wrath of God because of the evils inflicted on His Church.

Having said thus much as to the character of many of the alleged miracles of ecclesiastical history, it remains to say a few words —and they must be very few—as to the evidence by which they are substantiated. And (1) it is remarkable that we have in no case outside the New Testament got the

testimony of the person who is supposed to
have worked the miracles. There is no
instance whatever in which a writer claims
himself to have possession of supernatural
power—a very significant circumstance when
we recall the marked manner in which St.
Paul, *e.g.*, states that the gift of miracles
belonged to him. It may be remarked, in
passing, that this not only marks off the
miraculous of the New Testament from the
miracles of the mediæval Church, but it also
distinguishes the supernatural in Christianity
from the supernatural element in the other
great religions of the world. For neither
Mohammed nor Buddha ever pretended to
work wonders ; Mohammed, in the Koran,
says distinctly that he is a man like other
men ; and the strange and meaningless
mysteries with which Mohammedanism
abounds were, we know, fastened upon the
founder by later legends.[1] And in like manner the Buddhist legends teem with miserable

[1] Cf. for many references Paley, *Evidences*, Part
II. § 3.

miracles attributed to Buddha and his disciples, while Buddha himself prohibited the
working of wonders. We need not dwell
on the contrast here presented by Christianity ; for " the fact that Christ *professed*
to work miracles [in His own Person] is
established by evidence as ample as any
historical fact whatever." [1] And so when we
read of the extraordinary miracles attributed
to Gregory Thaumaturgus, we cannot fail
to be struck by the fact that they are not
mentioned in any writing of the saint himself—they are found in a biography written
a century after his death. Thus, too, the
life of Antony by Athanasius abounds in
miracle ; but here again the evidence is not
that of the principal person concerned, nor
is it even evidence contemporaneous with
the events. (2) In the next place, these
miracles attributed to saints may—in many
cases—be accounted for by the misguided
piety of their biographers. All too soon

---

[1] *Ecce Homo*, p. 40.

in the Church's history[1] a false criterion of sanctity grew up; it was supposed that the measure of a man's goodness was the amount of miraculous power by which his preaching was aided. Now from the belief that the man who works miracles must be a good man, the transition is easy to the converse inference. This man was a good man, as I know from my experience, therefore he must have worked miracles, and so it can be no harm to write down a few in his biography. He must have worked, if not these very wonders, at least others very like them.[2] We find thus that the farther removed in time the saint is from his biographer, the more is his life embellished with legend and glorified with miracle. The mediæval record therefore comes before us "a maimed and discredited authority"; we reject much of its contents on the above grounds, and so we look with hesitation on the rest. No cri-

---

[1] Cf. Mozley, *Bampton Lectures*, p. 181.

[2] Newman lays down a principle very like this. See *University Sermon on Development*, p. 345.

ticism of this sort can be applied to the miracles of the New Testament, for here we have contemporary testimony of the principal persons concerned ; and the miraculous is as prominent in the earlier as in the later canonical writings. (3) Thirdly, it inspires us with considerable doubt when we read how very opportunely many of these mediæval miracles happened—opportunely, that is, not so much for the welfare of Christianity as for the triumph of a particular party or the glorification of a particular individual. In one sense, indeed, it is very far from suspicious to read that a miracle came at the right moment, *i.e.* for the support of God's truth ; but in another sense it *is* suspicious. If men are anxiously expecting a sign from heaven to guarantee the piety of a doubtful undertaking or the success of a hazardous cause, it is very likely that they will see the finger of God in what is really only the operation of His ordinary laws, and it is not improbable that they may be the dupes of unscrupulous persons who play upon their

prejudices. *E.g.*, Ambrose tells a wonderful story, which is corroborated by Augustine, of miracles of healing wrought by the
relics of martyrs found under the high altar
of a church at Milan.[1] By the touch of
these sacred relics (which Ambrose says
he saw discovered with his own eyes) the
sick were relieved from their various diseases
—nay, even a blind man received his sight.
It may well be believed that this was told
in perfect good faith, but it does not follow
that the miraculous part of it is true. There
seems to be no doubt whatever that genuine

[1] Cf. Conf. ix. 16, Serm. 286, *De Civ. Dei*, xxii. 8;
and Ambr., Ep. 22. "Invenimus," says Ambrose,
"miræ magnitudinis viros duos, ut prisca ætas fere-
bat. Ossa omnia integra, sanguinis plurimum. . . .
Cognovistis, immo vidistis ipsi multos a dæmoniis pur-
gatos : plurimos etiam, ubi vestem sanctorum mani-
bus contigerunt, iis quibus laborabant, debilitatibus
absolutos : reparata vetusti temporis miracula, quo se
per adventum Domini Jesu gratia terris major infu-
derat, umbra quadam sanctorum corporum plerosque
anatos cernitis. Quanta oraria jactitantur ! Quanta
indumenta super reliquas sacratissimas et tactu ipso
medicabilia reposcuntur ! Gaudent omnes extrema
linea contingere, et qui contigerit, salvus erit."

12

relics of martyrs were discovered ; it has been shown recently that they are still preserved at Milan.[1] Now the natural enthusiasm resulting from such a discovery would incline men at that time to expect as a matter of course miraculous cures. They were immediately regarded as a party triumph. No one is likely to accuse Ambrose or Augustine of deliberate deceit, but it is far from unlikely that they should have been themselves deceived. Augustine, in especial, always had a hankering after miracle ; he seems to have been a regular collector of marvellous tales, which he has recorded, on several occasions innocently adding that few know of these miracles to which he alludes, and that those who do know are not impressed by them. He had[2] " that fervid sensitiveness towards whatever seems to connect humanity with a spiritual system which has been the char-

---

[1] On the whole subject of the relics at Milan, see Newman's *Hist. Sketches*, ii., p. 364, § 99, and a letter at the end of the volume from Father Ambrose St. John.

[2] Isaac Taylor, *Ancient Christianity.*

acteristic of many powerful minds"; on this ground we might name, in company with him, such men as Martin Luther and John Wesley. It is quite curious how Augustine has himself thrown doubt on his records of the miraculous by his comments. "The modern miracles," he says, "barely become known even to the population of the city or town in which they take place; and when recounted at a distance from the spot, they scarcely carry weight enough to get them believed without difficulty and hesitation, *even when reported by Christian people to Christian people.*" This failure to produce contemporary conviction gives us reason for supposing that the attestation was not so strong as the good bishop of Hippô supposed.

It would be quite beyond the limits of this lecture to enter more fully into the inadequacy of the mediæval testimony to miracle as compared with the apostolic. Thus much has been said, because it is often so confidently asserted that the one is as good, or nearly as good, as the other;

and also because it may be well to hint, however briefly, at the way in which such assertions should be met. They are often answered by arguments which, if valid, would destroy all belief in the miracles of the Gospel ; thus people sometimes try to over-throw the accounts of mediæval miracles by saying that they are contrary to the order of nature, and therefore *impossible*, and so there is no use in seriously reckoning with the testimony to them. But that argument, if valid, would destroy Christianity altogether; for if miracles be not *possible*, it is false. No ; the question is not one of possibility —miracles are always possible to any one who believes in a living God—it is entirely a question of evidence. And if we weigh it with care we shall be saved on the one hand from that enthusiasm for antiquity which imperils truth so seriously, and on the other from a negative scepticism which would deny the fact of a revelation of God to men in history.

LECTURE V.

THE LONG-LOST HARMONY.

By Rev. SAMUEL HEMPHILL, B.D.

LECTURE V.

THE LONG-LOST HARMONY.

THE natural man is determined not to accept the supernatural. But the life of Jesus embodies the supernatural. Therefore the natural man is determined not to accept the life of Jesus. He may very probably accept the moral teaching of Jesus, or at least part of it ; but the historical life of Jesus he will not accept.

It is at this point that Christianity and infidelity join issue. The historical life of Jesus is foolishness in the eyes of the natural man ; but for us Christians it is the very rock upon which all our hopes are built. We have been baptized into a personal and historical Jesus ; we have read and meditated on His words ; we have admired His acts ; 'we have turned the eye

of faith towards Him as hanging upon the
cross of Calvary for our sins; we have
rejoiced at His resurrection from the grave
in Joseph's garden; we have been assured
of His glorious ascension into heaven; and
regard Him as now representing and inter-
ceding for us there. Our Christianity is, in
short, bound up entirely and irrevocably in
the personal Jesus *of the Gospels;* and our
belief in Him is *founded* on our belief in *the
entirely historical character* of those ancient
records.

Now it is over half a century since Strauss
in Germany endeavoured to construct a "life
of Jesus" very different from that presented
in the Gospels: a "life" from which every
miraculous circumstance was rigidly elimi-
nated. His theory was that the accepted
account of Jesus was not historical, but a
parcel of myths about a shadowy personage.
The Gospels were treated by him as if they
were little better than romances, of a piece
with the legendary accounts of the infancy
and childhood of Jesus which go by the

name of "the apocryphal gospels," and the
so called "Clementine" fictions [1] about the
state of the early Christian Church. In
fact, the Gospels, according to Strauss, were
scarcely more historical than the Homeric
poems or the Scandinavian eddas.

This theory, which was at first the property
of a few in Germany, and rather tentatively
presented for acceptance in England and
other countries in a somewhat diluted form,
seems of late to have gained a fresh lease of
life, owing to the impetus which has been
given to the study of Oriental religions.

You are of course aware that, though
Buddha, Confucius, Zoroaster, and other
Oriental founders of religions were real persons, the accounts of their lives which are
to be found in their sacred books are by no
means historical, but contain a vast amount
of legendary matter.

[1] *The Clementine Recognitions* are translated in
the third volume of T. & T. Clark's "Ante-Nicene
Christian Library," and the *Clementine Homilies* in
the eighteenth volume of the same series.

Now the happy thought struck some modern leaders of the attack on Christianity, that the history of Jesus is, after all, only of the same character as the traditional accounts of these Oriental founders of religions ; that they are all equally true and equally false ; and that, in short, a large body of legend and myth has attached itself to the name of an historical person, Jesus of Nazareth, who, like His Eastern rivals (or brethren !), went about doing good, and preaching His peculiar system of ethics ; who in due course fell a victim to the intolerance of His fellow countrymen, and after His death somehow got to be regarded as a God by His ignorant and fanatical followers.

We in Ireland have an instance of this accretion of myth round the person of a religious teacher, in the popular account of St. Patrick.

No one doubts that there was such a person as Patrick, that he lived and taught in Ireland, and that his date was the middle of the fifth century.

But later ages have each supplied their

contribution of myth; and the popular "lives" of the saint now current amongst the less educated classes of our countrymen have about as strong claim to be regarded as sober history as have the *Idylls of the King.*

Now it is very important that we should remember that in cases where mythical stories gather round the name of an historical personage, this always happens long after his death. First, some real event in the life of the great man is exaggerated, and the door is thus opened for the entrance of the miraculous element; then similar miraculous stories are boldly invented, or stories that have long been current in the folk-lore of the country are attributed to the hero whom all delight to honour.

From my home in the country I can plainly see the precipice from which the legend declares that Patrick drove all the snakes and toads into the nether regions; yet seeing is not believing, and for this simple reason, that I know the legend was not current until some hundreds of years after the poor saint's bones had crumbled into dust at Saul, near Downpatrick.

In the same way writers of the modern infidel or semi-infidel school allege that the miracles recounted in the Gospels are mere myths, like the accretions which the ocean of time has deposited round the names, let us say, of Buddha and St. Patrick. The Gospels, therefore, which contain this calcareous deposit of myth must have come into their present shape long ages after the time when Jesus lived upon the earth. And this is now the well-defined battleground between belief and unbelief. The assailants of Christianity find themselves obliged to assign the composition of the Gospels to a late date, so as to allow for the growth of the mythical element ; and so they allege that the title deeds of our faith were not written until the end of the second century.

Perhaps some of you wonder why they do not allow more time than this, and put the composition of the Gospels to a still later date, say the end of the third or fourth century.

Well, be assured that they would dearly like to do so, but they cannot, because three celebrated Church writers who lived about the end of the second century—Irenæus, Clement of Alexandria, and Tertullian—make such frequent and copious use of our Gospels in their extant writings, which are very voluminous, that even the wildest sceptic cannot deny that these Gospels existed in their present form in the time of the aforesaid Fathers.

Now it is my aim in the two lectures assigned to me to push the date of the composition of the Gospels back from the end of the second century, when sceptics allow that they existed, to within measurable distance of the actual time when Christ lived upon the earth. I shall produce incontestable proof that our Gospels existed in their present form, to say the least, near the beginning of the second century, or in other words, within a few years of the lifetime of John, the last survivor of the group who " saw and heard and handled " the actual Person Jesus. Thus the mythical theory will be squeezed out for want of

room to breathe in ; and you will see that
the life of Jesus differs from the accounts of
Buddha, Confucius, Zoroaster and the others,
in this most vital particular, that it is drawn
from histories which are all but contemporaneous with the person about whom they treat.

But before examining any such evidence,
it is our duty to remember that but few
fragments of very early Christian literature
have come down to us. So that we are not
to be surprised if some things are brought
forward which at first sight may seem insignificant. Amid the general wreck of
early Church literature may no doubt be
reckoned many allusions to the fourfold
life of Jesus. But though much evidence
has doubtless perished, through the ravages
of time, yet sufficient remains, in the providence of God, to confirm us in our most holy
faith, and to furnish a weapon by which we
can unhorse our assailants.

By fixing the composition of our Gospels
at the end of the second century, sceptical
critics have ignored a work which has always

been known *by name* in the Church as the *Diatessaron of Tatian.* In fact, the allusions to this work which have been gleaned from the scanty remains of early Christian literature reach back as far as the first quarter of the fourth century, when Eusebius, the learned and accurate historian, wrote a notice of it. It was mentioned subsequently by Epiphanius and Theodoret ;[1] and the latter was quite familiar with its form and character, for he found and examined over two hundred copies of it, in the diocese of Cyrrhus near the Euphrates, of which he was bishop A.D. 453.

Now let it be noted at the outset that these three writers, Eusebius, Epiphanius, and Theodoret, however they may have differed in their knowledge of the book and their estimate of its value, stated plainly and precisely, not only that it existed in their time, but that it was compiled by the celebrated

---

[1] References will be found in Lightfoot's *Essays on Supernatural Religion*, Salmon's *Introduction to the New Testament*, and my *Diatessaron of Tatian*, to which books the student is once for all referred.

apologist Tatian, the friend and pupil of Justin Martyr. Of this Tatian we fortunately know a great deal, because we have his *Apology*,[1] which, it seems, he composed at Rome, not long after the middle of the second century. Those of you who have studied Justin Martyr's first Apology will understand that it was the practice of the advocates who in early times held a brief for Christianity to devote a large share of their attention to discredit the deities then worshipped at Rome and elsewhere. Tatian revels in this part of his task. His powers of ridicule and satire seem inexhaustible, and serve to portray the man as bold and incautious to a wonderful degree. Tatian also gives a short sketch of his own life up to the time when the Apology was composed. He recounts the fact that he was by birth an Assyrian, that is, a native of the country to the east of the Tigris, but which had been

[1] An English translation of this most interesting apology is contained in the third volume of T. & T. Clark's "Ante-Nicene Christian Library."

included by Trajan in the Roman province of Syria. Throughout this province the vernacular was Syriac, but as there were many Greek-speaking merchants and officials there, Greek must have been well understood by the more educated classes of the community. Tatian, at any rate, was trained in Greek literature, of which he was a diligent student. He also, like some others, as Justin and Theophilus, who afterwards became defenders of the Christian faith, on reaching manhood sought earnestly for some guide to teach him about the true God, and show him where he could find rest for his weary soul.

According to his own account, he travelled from one country to another, but got satisfaction from no man. The heathen mysteries into which he had been initiated disgusted him by their revolting and licentious rites. He got to hate with perfect hatred those who were reputed to be gods ; and to despise from the bottom of his heart those who called themselves philosophers, on account of their covetousness. He was, like Mohammed,

13

a wandering searcher after light and truth; but unlike Mohammed in that he found them. He happened to fall in with the Sacred Scriptures [1] (doubtless of the Old Testament). He read. He was delighted with the artless grandeur of their style. This, as long afterwards in Luther's case, began by attracting, and ended by convincing him. Nor did he fail to notice, as Justin had also noticed, that these Scriptures were far older than any of the heathen writings.

The result was that he became an ardent Christian, and making his way to the imperial city of Rome, attached himself to the school of Justin, whose lectures he attended, and whose persecutions he shared, even to the imminent peril of his life.

Such are the gleanings which we can gather about the first part of Tatian's career. Imagination may perhaps be allowed tentatively to fill up the outline. We can think of

[1] He calls them the "barbaric writings" in his Apology, as this is the name which his heathen readers or hearers would understand.

the close companionship of the two teachers ;
we can follow them into their secluded re-
fuge, perhaps in the famous catacombs ; we
can think of how, like Paul and Silas, they
must have cheered one another, in times of
peril, by prayer and praise, and the remembrance of the words and works of their master Jesus ; until at last they parted, one to
drink the cup of martyrdom in this life, the
other to hatch some unlucky opinion which
would, like an avenging fury, pursue and
blacken his memory through seventeen long
centuries of posthumous martyrdom.

After the death of the elder apologist,
Tatian seems, from the little we can learn
of him, to have continued for a time at
Rome, where it is probable that he numbered
among his pupils Clement, who afterwards
became famous as the head of the great
Christian school of Alexandria, and who
has been already mentioned as one of the
witnesses to the four Gospels at the end of
the second century. During this residence
at Rome Tatian probably wrote the greater

number of his once numerous works, such
as those on problems connected with the
hidden and obscure things of the Old
Testament, on Christian perfection, and on
the epistles of St. Paul. All these have
been lost, or, to speak more correctly, belong
to the yet undiscovered mass of early literature, so that we can hazard no opinion upon
their nature or tendency. But if we are to
be guided by what subsequent writers have
recorded, we must come to the conclusion
that Tatian developed some offensive and
questionable opinions, and forfeited his fair
fame as an orthodox Christian. The early
Fathers at any rate are unanimous in de-
nouncing him as a heretic, though they
disagree as to the cause. Clement of Alexandria, who had probably been his pupil,
said that he regarded marriage as a sin ;
and certainly we must all admit that it
would be unfortunate if such an opinion
should gain wide acceptance! But it appears
that Tatian did not stop even there, for
Clement adds that he also committed him-

self to the unpardonable prediction that beautiful hair and other adornments would entail punishment on their fair possessors!

And passing to more theological but scarcely less speculative topics, we find that Irenæus charged him with holding that Adam was not saved ; and that Origen said that he regarded God's words, " Let there be light," as a prayer. And when we come to Jerome, we find that lapse of time had done nothing to soften the distasteful epithets which were applied to poor Tatian, and that the monk of Bethlehem was able to supply a vocabulary more than sufficient for his purpose !

You have already heard that Tatian was a native of the Roman province of Syria, and it appears from Epiphanius that it was in that country that he ended his days, engaged, as we may fervently hope, in preaching the blessed Gospel to his still heathen countrymen. We must suppose either that he had been excommunicated by the church of Rome for his heretical writings and teach-ings, or that he had voluntarily retired from a sphere in which he felt that his power for good was gone. The proud and defiant author of the *Apology* was not the man to brook opposition, or to mince matters with his orthodox censors ; and we can well imagine the scornful farewell which he bade to the Church which he believed had treated him badly. At any rate, we have no choice but to hold that Epiphanius, our only informant, is right when he tells us that Tatian retired, after his Roman experiences, to the banks of the Euphrates.

Such is the man to whom the authorship of the *Diatessaron* is attributed by Eusebius, Epiphanius, and Theodoret (not to mention later writers), and it now becomes our duty to inquire into the nature and contents of this, up to a recent date, shadowy and unknown work.

The statement of Eusebius is as follows :

" Tatian composed a sort of connexion and compilation, I know not how, of the Gospels, and called it the *Diatessaron*. This work is current in some quarters even to the present day."

From this we learn that the work in question was compiled out of "the Gospels," which were as well known in Eusebius' time as in our own. And we can understand why the name "Diatessaron" should have been given to it, inasmuch as that is the Greek for "by the four." Indeed, the full title of the book as given by Epiphanius was "The Diatessaron Gospel," and as given by Theodoret, "The Gospel which is called Diatessaron." So that it was impossible for Christian writers to resist the inference that a kind of patchwork, composed of pieces of the four canonical Gospels, was current in the early Church ; and that it was composed by Tatian, who, as we have seen, flourished in the time of Justin Martyr, or about the middle of the second century.

It may be well, perhaps, to remark in passing, that the compilation of passages from the four canonical Gospels into one connected narrative has not been unknown in more recent times. The sisters of Little Gidding in the seventeenth century spent many of their leisure hours in this work;[1] and a specimen of their harmonizing skill was a few years ago exhibited in Dublin at the Decorative Art Exhibition. And even so late as A.D. 1888 Mr. Frederic F. Hamilton published at Paris a French compilation of a very complete character, with the title *L'Évangile des Évangiles.*

But to return to our subject. The sceptical school, in fixing the composition of the Gospels at the end of the second century, inadvertently or designedly omitted to notice the immense difficulty under which their speculations laboured, owing to these and other historical references to a compilation from the four Gospels made by a man who cannot have been born much later than A.D. 120, or twenty years after the death of John who leaned on Jesus' breast at supper. But as Christian writers were

---

[1] A pleasant and sympathetic account of them is given in *John Inglesant*, by Mr. Shorthouse.

not slow to produce these references in evidence, it became necessary for their opponents to face the difficulty, and it will doubtless entertain you to know what they had to say about the *Diatessaron.*

Some affirmed that as the word " Diatessaron " was a term borrowed from Greek music, it only implied perfect harmony, without necessary limitation to four. But the derivation may just as likely be from medicine, where " Diatessaron " means a compound of four ingredients, as has been lately proved.[1]

But I must quote some statements from a trashy book called *Supernatural Religion,* which was quite the rage amongst English sceptics some years ago.

" There is therefore no authority for saying that Tatian's Gospel was a harmony of four Gospels at all, and the name ' Diatessaron ' was not only not given by Tatian himself to the work, but was merely the usual fore-

---

[1] By Dr. Quarry, see Salmon's *Introduction*, p. 83, ed. 4.

gone conclusion of the Christians of the third and fourth centuries that everything in the shape of evangelical literature must be dependent on the Gospels adopted by the Church." [1]

And again :

"No one seems to have seen Tatian's Harmony, probably for the very simple reason that there was no such work." [2]

And again :

"It is obvious that there is no evidence whatever connecting Tatian's Gospel with those in our canon." [3]

I think that the thing which will soon be really obvious to us all is that the person who thus ignores the plain statements of credible historians like Eusebius and Theodoret merely puts himself out of court.

Now remember that the two points which are here denied are, first, that a compilation

[1] Complete ed., vol. ii., p. 154, changes " merely " into " probably."

[2] Complete ed., p. 156.

[3] Complete ed., vol. ii., p. 157, changes " whatever " into " of any value."

of the four Gospels ever existed which would answer to the description of Eusebius ; and, second, that any such compilation had a right to be attributed to Tatian. We shall soon be able to test the value of these denials.

Up to the present I have told you only a little of what Eusebius, Epiphanius, and Theodoret said about the *Diatessaron;* but I have not yet indicated the quarter from which the most copious information comes to us on the subject.

It is only lately that any but a very small minority of scholars have given much attention to the study of Oriental Christian literature. The generality seemed too well satisfied with the treasures of Latin and Greek Church writers to turn their thoughts towards the vast Oriental resources which enterprise had put within their reach. And to this must be attributed the ignorance of the *Diatessaron* which prevailed so generally until a few years ago. The Greek and Latin Church writers were ransacked for some further information about the lost Harmony, but none was forthcoming.

Though an anonymous Harmony in Latin,
which answered to the description of Eusebius, had indeed been found and edited by
Victor, Bishop of Capua, in the middle of
the sixth century, and though he had
conjectured that it was none other than the
Diatessaron of Tatian, yet it has never, till
quite lately, been proved whether he was
right or wrong. Indeed, it was generally
assumed by those who wrote on the subject
at all, that Victor had made a mistake. But
be that as it may, except for this one conjecture, which seemed incapable of verifica-
tion, Western Christian literature furnished
no clue to the *Diatessaron.*

But on turning our attention to the
literature of the East, we are able to fill the
void which has so long been the *crux* of
orthodox critics.

You will recollect that Tatian was born in
a country whose vernacular was Syriac, and
that it was to this country that he retreated
after he left Rome. You will also recollect
that Theodoret is the only one of the early

Fathers who mentions the *Diatessaron* as a book with which he was thoroughly acquainted. Now Theodoret was the bishop of a diocese in which Syriac was the vernacular, and it will therefore not surprise you to be told that it is to Syriac literature that we must go for the clue to this interesting problem. At any rate, history begins to find her voice the moment we touch Syrian soil ; and we seem to have at last traced the long-lost Harmony to its source.

But it will be convenient for you, in the first place, to learn the exact words of Theodoret himself.

"He (Tatian) composed the Gospel which is called 'Diatessaron,' cutting out the genealogies and such other passages as show the Lord to have been born of the seed of David after the flesh. This work was in use not only among persons belonging to his sect, but also among those who follow the apostolic doctrine, as they did not perceive the mischief of the composition, but used the book in all simplicity on account of its brevity. And I myself found more than two hundred such copies held in respect in the churches in our parts. All these I collected and put away, and I replaced them by the Gospels of the four evangelists."[1]

Here are the statements of an eye-witness, who was perfectly familiar with the book, who had handled many copies of it, and had minutely examined its contents. And this witness, who was a man of vast reputation as a writer of candour and scholarship, and who was well acquainted with the past history of his Church, accepted it as an undoubted fact that the book had been compiled by Tatian. Indeed, it is not at all unlikely that this very circumstance, that it was the unquestioned work of Tatian the heretic, was a more serious blemish in the eyes of the zealous bishop than any internal

---

[1] Lightfoot's renderings are nearly always adopted. Dr. Dale, *The Living Christ and the Four Gospels*, pp. 156, 158, inadvertently attributes translations to me, which I (*Diatessaron*, p. xiv., note 1) had stated were adopted from Lightfoot's Essay.

defect, such as the omission of our Lord's genealogies; and that he acted in very much the same manner as a Romish bishop in Ireland would act at the present day, if he were to suppress the Protestant Bible throughout his diocese on account of its Protestant associations, rather than for any imperfection of rendering which he might perceive in it.

We can easily picture for ourselves the scenes which must have taken place when Theodoret and his archdeacon and other subordinates went round the eight hundred parishes of the diocese of Cyrrhus, seeking for the old Harmony, and confiscating it, to the infinite chagrin of the simple parish priests and their simpler flocks, who had been accustomed from infancy to hear from its pages the story of redeeming love. It must indeed have been endeared to them as an old-fashioned Church book, which their fathers and grandfathers had fondly venerated, and which was the subject of many stories of the early days of Syrian Christianity.

Of these stories a specimen may be found in a curious old Syriac writing, which was brought to light A.D. 1864. It is called the *Doctrine of Addai,* and it gives a kind of legendary history of the founding of the Church at Edessa, in the time of good King Abgar. I must quote the words which bear on our subject : [1]

"And they ministered in the church which Addai had built at the order and command of King Abgar, and they were furnished with what belonged to the king and to his nobles with some things for the house of God, and others for the supply of the poor. But a large multitude of people assembled day by day, and came to the prayers of the service, and to the reading of the Old Testament and the New of the *Diatessaron.*"

It is not necessary for us to regard this account as strictly historical, indeed it reads more like an historical romance ; but it does

[1] From Cureton's *Ancient Syriac Documents.* (London, 1864.)

not follow that its evidence is therefore worthless. There are many interesting historical details to be learned from Sir Walter Scott's novels ; indeed, it was the object of that writer to preserve strict *verisimilitude* in all his stories. And we may be sure that the traditions and customs which he records had a real existence amongst the people to whom he attributes them. In the same way, the least that can be said about the *Doctrine of Addai* is, that at the time of its composition the *Diatessaron* must have been the form in which the Gospel was commonly read at daily service in the Syrian churches with which the writer was familiar. And, as the romance may perhaps date back as early as the third century, this would prove that for at least one hundred years the *Diatessaron* had been a well-known book among the Syrians ; and that many ages before the visitation when Bishop Theodoret went round his diocese to suppress it, the simple country-folk (like Englishmen at the time of the

14

Reformation) had been accustomed to gather round and drink in attentively the words of eternal life which were read from its pages, as it lay upon the desk of their rural sanctuary.

Nor was the use of the *Diatessaron* confined to the less educated members of the Church. Two great figures shine out brightly in the Syrian ecclesiastical history of the fourth century—Aphraates, "the Persian Sage," who was a great teacher at Mossul (Nineveh) about A.D. 340; and Ephraem, "the Harp of the Holy Spirit," so called for his eminence as a hymn-writer, who lived and laboured at Edessa, about twenty years later.

The lamented Professor William Wright, well known in our University, in his edition of the *Homilies of Aphraates*, published A.D. 1869, remarked this author's practice of "mixing up the words of two or more passages of Scripture" in his citation of texts; and Professor Zahn, in what must be regarded as the classical work on the *Diates-*

saron, which he published A.D. 1881,[1] has satisfactorily demonstrated that these composite citations of Aphraates are due to his habitual use of Tatian's Harmony.

But the case of Ephraem is even more striking. Remember that he taught at Edessa, a town in the neighbourhood of which it is possible that Tatian preached after his return from Rome. And so great was his fame that Gregory of Nyssa could say in his funeral oration that the splendour of his life and teaching had shone throughout the whole world : an encomium which we can quite understand, when we consider not only the deep spirituality of his hymns and expositions which we still have,[2] but the surprisingly voluminous nature of his works which were once extant.[3]

You will, however, be disappointed to learn that Ephraem, though estimable in almost

---

[1] At Erlangen.

[2] See *Select Metrical Hymns and Homilies of Ephraem Syrus*, translated from the Syriac by the Rev. H. Burgess, Ph.D. (London, 1853.)

[3] Three million lines (Sozomen, *E. H.* iii. 16).

every other way, was by no means an admirer of the fair sex. Though connected with the divinity school of Edessa, we have no record that he ever lectured to an audience of young ladies. It is true that Edessa was perhaps not so fortunate as to contain an institution like the Alexandra College; but in any case Ephraem would hardly have felt quite at his ease before an audience of ladies, as you may judge from the following anecdote, which is related of his entrance into Edessa.[1]

"As he entered the city, a number of women were engaged in washing linen on the banks of the river Daisan, and as one of them looked at him more intently than seemed becoming, he rebuked her, saying, 'Be modest, O woman, and fix thy look upon the ground.' 'It is quite right,' she answered, 'for men to look upon the ground, for out of it they were taken; but for the same reason I may surely look at thee, for

[1] See Dean Payne Smith's article EPHRAEM, in Smith's *Dictionary of Christian Biography.*

woman was taken out of man.' 'If the women here,' he said, as he passed on, 'are so wise, what must the men be?'"

But if Ephraem delivered no lectures to young women, he is believed to have delivered many to young men. Indeed, there is good reason to suppose that a large portion of the matter which he has left in the form of commentaries on the Scriptures came to be composed originally for the instruction of his class of divinity students.

Now the connexion of Ephraem with the *Diatessaron* of Tatian is a point of the greatest interest. For many centuries it has been believed that he wrote an exposition of the Gospel narrative, taking the *Diatessaron* as his basis; and this tradition has been recorded by many Syrian writers. The first and greatest of these, from whom indeed the others seem to have copied, is Dionysius Bar-Salîbi, who was bishop of Amida in the closing years of the twelfth century, and whose own commentary on the Gospels is now very highly valued by Syriac scholars. In the preface to his commentary on St. Mark, Bar-Salîbi writes as follows :

" Tatian, the disciple of Justin, the philosopher and martyr, selected and patched together from the four Gospels, and constructed a Gospel, which he called ' Diatessaron,' that is *Miscellanies.* On this work Mar Ephraem wrote an exposition ; and its commencement was, ' *In the beginning was the Word.*' " [1]

It is hard to imagine a statement more explicit than this, or more calculated to convince reasonable minds. It was made with the utmost deliberation by a writer of learning and credit ; but the opponents of orthodox Christianity thought themselves justified in ignoring it on the ground of the lateness of the testimony. The irrational nature of this treatment was ably shown by the lamented Bishop (then Professor) Lightfoot, in an article in the *Contemporary Review,* May, 1877, in which Bar-Salîbi was held to

[1] Lightfoot's version.

be "worthy of all credit," in his statement that Ephraem wrote a commentary on the *Diatessaron* of Tatian.

And this conclusion of our great English theologian was soon splendidly verified by the appearance of the commentary itself, which, as a matter of fact, had already been published in a Latin form at Venice, A.D. 1876, but did not make its way to England till some years after.

As this is one of the most interesting and valuable contributions to theology made in the present century, you will like to hear a few particulars about it.

The medium through which it came was the to us almost entirely unknown Armenian language. You have perhaps heard that the monastery of San Lazzaro at Venice, founded almost two centuries ago by an Armenian priest named Mechitar, has ever since remained the focus of Armenian learning and culture. It contains a valuable collection of ancient Armenian manuscripts, including a Ritual of the eighth century;

the Bible of Melké, Queen of Armenia,
written in the year 902; and last, but not
least, two twelfth century copies of an Armenian version, made apparently in the fifth
century from the Syriac, of Ephraem's commentary on a Gospel Harmony.

The monks have a printing press of their
own, and over half a century ago (A.D. 1836)
printed an Armenian edition of St. Ephraem's
works, which contained the commentary on
the Gospel Harmony. Moreover, a Latin
translation of this last was made so long ago
as A.D. 1841 by Father Aucher, who is well
known in connexion with the Armenian
version of the Bible; but this Latin version
remained in manuscript until Professor
Moesinger of Salzburg had the distinguished
honour of revising and publishing it, A.D.
1876.

Such is a brief sketch of the history of this
most opportune publication, which a few
years ago caused a general panic in the
sceptical camp. It is impossible on the
present occasion to enter into any detailed

criticism of its internal character, but I may mention that competent scholars have satisfied themselves on the following points :

(1) That the Armenian work is a rather servile version of a Syriac original made about the fifth century.

(2) That internal evidence conclusively points to Ephraem as the author.

(3) That the basis of the commentary is a Gospel Harmony, such as would fully answer to the description of Eusebius and Theodoret.

The irresistible conclusion therefore is that this is the very commentary mentioned by Dionysius Bar-Salîbi ; and that its basis was the very *Diatessaron* mentioned by Eusebius, Theodoret, the author of the *Doctrine of Addai*, and others.

We have a common proverb that " it never rains but it pours," and this has been verified in the case of the *Diatessaron.* For no sooner had theologians recast their methods of dealing with the Tatian controversy, consequent on the appearance of Moesinger's book, than they were again

startled by the publication at Rome, A.D.
1888, of the *Diatessaron* itself in the form
of an Arabic translation made in the eleventh
century from the Syriac. The editor of this
work was Father Ciasca, of the Vatican
Library, one of the greatest living Coptic
scholars ; and he not only subjoined a Latin
version of the Arabic, but wrote an interesting preface giving an account of the occasion
and reason of the publication, and of the
manuscripts from which the text was drawn.

It is unnecessary for us to do more than
notice that one of the manuscripts contains
notes at the beginning and end in which the
reader is informed that he has before him
an Arabic translation of Tatian's *Diatessaron*,
that it was made from the Syriac, and that
the translator was "the most learned pres-
byter Abû-l-Pharag Abdullah Ben-at-Tîb."

Comparing the Latin version of this
Arabic *Diatessaron* with the Latin version
of the fragments of the Harmony which
Ephraem used, we cannot for a moment
doubt that they represent the very same

original compilation. Further, we are able without difficulty to restore that compilation, so as to learn the principle upon which it was made, the materials of which it was composed, and the type of text to which it belonged.

So much for the recovery of the *Diatessaron*. Let me now briefly recapitulate the evidence for connecting it with Tatian; for that is the point of our present inquiry.

1. We have the *negative* evidence that only two [1] *Diatessarons*, those of Tatian and Ammonius, are mentioned in extant Church literature, or were discoverable by Victor, the learned bishop of Capua, in the sixth century.

And as the present Harmony differs in principle and detail from the *Diatessaron* of Ammonius, as described by Eusebius, while it agrees with the *Diatessaron* of Tatian, as described by several writers, it is only reasonable to infer that this Harmony is the *Diatessaron* of Tatian.

---

[1] Bar-Salîbi speaks of a third, otherwise unknown, by Elias of Salamia. See Lightfoot's *Essays*, p. 280.

2. And Bar-Salîbi is absolutely conclusive on this point ; for he distinctly states that Tatian compiled the Harmony upon which Ephraem wrote a commentary, and the present work is that Harmony.

3. Independent witness to Tatian's authorship is also found in the notes at the beginning and end of the Arabic edition of the same Harmony.

4. And this authorship by one who was a Syrian, not only by birth, but by residence during the later years of his life, accords with the traditional reading of the *Diatessaron* at the founding of the Church of Edessa ; its use by Aphraates, the great preacher of Mossul, and by Ephraem, the poet and commentator of Edessa ; its wide circulation throughout the diocese of Cyrrhus ; its textual resemblance to the old Syriac Gospels edited by Cureton ; its translation from Syriac into Arabic in the eleventh century ; and, in a word, its exclusively Syrian history.

We have thus maintained our two points

that the *Diatessaron* existed, and that it was compiled by Tatian.

Now recollect that the *Diatessaron* is a patchwork composed of pieces of our four Gospels, and of them alone ; and that for the purpose of forming a connected narrative of the life of our Lord, this teacher in the second century was in precisely the same position as the Sisters of Little Gidding in the seventeenth. The four Gospels therefore, which held an unique and revered position in the seventeenth century, held exactly the same position in the third quarter of the second century. They were at that early date in undisputed possession of the field, as the only authentic form of apostolic tradition. The statement therefore that they were composed in their present form at or near the end of the second century can no longer be made by any one who cares to avoid the imputation of downright ignorance.

LECTURE VI.

EARLY VESTIGES OF THE FOURFOLD GOSPEL.

By Rev. SAMUEL HEMPHILL, B.D.

LECTURE VI.

EARLY VESTIGES OF THE FOURFOLD GOSPEL.

A SHORT time ago, as I was travelling in the train, a friend kindly handed me a shilling volume in which the chief religions of the world were described and compared, Christianity being considerately given a place with the systems of Buddha, Zoroaster, Confucius, and others; something like the way in which the Roman emperor, Alexander Severus, allowed our Lord's statue a place near those of Jupiter, Mercury, and the other classical divinities. Glancing at the title-page, I saw that the little book had already run through ten editions (and, for all I know, it may now have run through ten more); and then turning to the rather subordinate chapter which dealt with the Christian

Gospels, I gained the interesting information that these records had been composed at the end of the second century.

Now it is quite possible that some of you have seen, or may see, such a book ; and therefore it will not be out of place to lay a few hard facts before you, which will enable you effectively to criticise the cavalier manner in which the title-deeds of our faith are treated in these sceptical productions, which seem to have gained the ear of a portion of the thinking public.

We have already considered the *Diatessaron* of Tatian, the compilation of portions of our four Gospels which was made by a celebrated teacher who flourished at Rome somewhere about the middle of the second century.

I must however tell you that the compilation of the *Diatessaron* belongs probably to the close of Tatian's career, after he had for ever left the great Western capital, and buried himself among the wild heathen people of the East ; and therefore we must follow Zahn, the great German specialist, in placing its date somewhere about A.D. 172.

So that, even according to this estimate, in which we allow our opponents the full length of tether to which they can possibly be entitled, the four Gospels which we now have were harmonized into a single narrative, probably for the sake of instructing Tatian's Syrian converts, *about thirty years before they were composed*, according to sceptical shilling books !

But the materials of a patchwork must have come into being, not *after*, but *before* the patchwork itself. The richly variegated counterpanes which are such a pleasing feature in the cottages of our peasant neighbours are evidently composed of pieces of calico and other materials which have already done service in some other capacity. The shells and pebbles which we see embedded in the matrix of a conglomerate rock must first have had a separate existence, washed by the waves on some prehistoric sea-shore.

And according to the same universal law,

it is evident that the four Gospels, out of which a patchwork was made in or about A.D. 172, cannot have been themselves composed that year, but must have existed years before. We must allow sufficient time to enable these various records, emanating as they evidently did from various countries, to have been written, published, disseminated through the world, brought together, studied by Tatian, and recognised by him as the exclusively authentic form of apostolic tradition. They must have been sufficiently long in the world to have outstripped all rival records, and established their own unique character.

Now it is hard to believe that all this could have taken place in one decade, or even two. It generally takes a few years for a book now-a-days to become widely and popularly known, even with all the modern machinery of advertising and reviewing. And this was even more true of the early days, before the invention of printing ; and more especially with books which were not popular, but belonged to a sect which was everywhere spoken against.

We conclude therefore that the four Gospels cannot have been very new when Tatian compiled his *Diatessaron* out of them. And we feel justified in pushing them back, provisionally at least, to A.D. 150.

But perhaps you say, " This date, which the lecturer now assigns to the Gospels, is nearly 120 years after the events of the life of Jesus, and probably eighty years after the time at which we were taught to believe that these records were written ; and it is about half a century after the death of St. John, the last of the apostles."

Now all this may be admitted, and yet we may hold that it would not necessarily invalidate the authenticity of the Gospels. For we may legitimately urge that, though we could not *trace* them to an earlier date than A.D. 150, yet that would not prove that they did not exist earlier. Moreover, we may remind you that the larger part of the Christian literature of the second century has perished, and that this fact is enough to account for the lack of definite and full information about the early reception of the Gospels. And, finally, we may cry out against the unfairness of demanding documentary attestation of the Gospels, greater in amount and earlier in date than would be demanded in the case of any secular writer. The learned Provost of Trinity College, Dublin, in his *Introduction to the Books of the New Testament*,[1] gives an interesting example of this. He notices that the plays of Terence are quoted by Cicero and Horace, and that we require neither more nor earlier witnesses. Yet Cicero and Horace wrote a hundred years after Terence. So that it is unfair of those who receive the witness of Cicero and Horace to Terence to refuse to accept similar evidence to the Gospels.

But we are not obliged to stand on our

[1] To this work, and to Lightfoot's *Essays*, the student is referred for information about the use of the Gospels by Justin and Papias. Westcott, *Canon of the New Testament*, should also be consulted.

strict rights in this matter. Fortunately, in spite of the almost general wreck of early Church literature, the wise providence of God has left us some very interesting and very plain vestiges of the fourfold Gospel, which I shall now endeavour to present briefly to your notice.

We have already conjectured that the Gospels out of which Tatian made his compilation about A.D. 172 must have existed at least twenty years before. I have now to verify this conjecture, and *prove* that in point of fact they were used by a celebrated Church writer about that date.

You remember that Tatian was the friend and pupil of Justin Martyr ; that they lived and taught in the same city of Rome, were persecuted by the same adversaries, shared the same dangers. Is it not natural then to expect that the same records of the life and words of Jesus which Tatian knew and used were known also to Justin, and used by him in his literary labours ?

Fortunately we have sufficient material

from which to draw a pretty full account of Justin's life ; for three authentic works of his are in our hands, his two *Apologies*, and his *Dialogue* with the Jew Trypho ; and these documents furnish the following sketch of his history :

He lived at Neapolis, the ancient Shechem, and was, as he himself says, a Samaritan— not indeed by race or religion, but by residence. As we saw in the case of Tatian, Justin was skilled in Greek literature ; like Tatian too, he set out in search of a creed which could satisfy the cravings of his soul. First he applied to a Stoic teacher, but quickly transferred his attention to a Peripatetic. The latter soon overshot the mark by demanding payment for his instructions ; and Justin tried a Pythagorean. But he gave the discouraging information that it would be necessary for Justin to learn music, astronomy, and geometry, before he could learn about God. The soul of a seeker after truth is naturally impatient of delay, and so Justin next tried a follower of Plato, from whom he

learned a surer and better philosophy. He
tells us that "the contemplation of the *Ideas*
gave wings to his mind," and that he used
often to seek solitary places, in which he
could meditate on the deep truths which he
had been taught. When, one day, walking
on the sea-shore, he met an old man, who
began to question him on the higher life;
and finding that his soul was still unsatisfied,
pointed him to Christ. Justin felt that it
was philosophy which had thus led him to
his Saviour; and he was the more impressed
with Christianity on account of the unworld-
liness of its adherents, and their bravery
when subjected by the authorities to the
most cruel persecutions.

We are told that henceforth, under the
garb of the philosopher, he played the part
of the Christian advocate. Like Paul, he
held discussions in the public places, and
in a private residence. The *Dialogue* with
Trypho may serve to give us some idea of
the method of his reasoning; and the two
Apologies, composed in the reign of Antoninus

Pius (the first dating from about A.D. 150), display his fearless advocacy of the cause which he had embraced.

Let us leave Church history to finish the story of Justin's life, and to chronicle his martyrdom, while we turn to his extant writings to find out whether they can throw any light on the early reception of our four Gospels.

Now, in the first place, it must be noted that Justin constantly quotes the words and acts of the Saviour's life from *a written source.* He constantly uses the word γέ-γραπται (it is written) when referring to some circumstance about the life of Jesus. Now the use of this word γέγραπται implies much, for it is the word which the Saviour Himself used when pointing to the passages of the Old Testament which referred to His person. The presumption therefore is, that Justin placed the written source from which he got his information on somewhat the same footing as the Old Testament Scriptures, which holy men of God spake and wrote as they were borne along by the Holy Ghost.

Our next point is, that this written source of information which Justin used seems to have contained exactly what our present Gospels contain. If the creed of Justin be pieced together from what he says of the Saviour, drawing his information from this written source, the result will be found to be that, except for two or three exceedingly minute points, he never travels beyond our present Gospels. He knows only what we know. The presumption then is, that his written source of information was at least similar to ours.

But another remarkable fact is also clear. The written source which Justin quotes for his facts about the Saviour's life is not one homogeneous book, but *several* books, and to these he gives the name *Gospels*, and says that they were written by " the apostles."

Now this is a point well worthy of attention, for sceptical critics have eagerly taken hold of the fact that Justin generally calls

his written source of information *Memoirs.*
We must admit that this is his usual and
oft-reiterated name; but under the circumstances, is it not quite natural? Remember,
that in the three books of Justin which have
come down to us, he is dealing with those
outside the Church, those who are opponents
of Christianity. Now what more natural
than that he should employ a general and
vulgar word, which every one would understand, in order to convey to these Jewish
and heathen adversaries some idea of what
he was talking about? Justin had reached
Christianity through philosophy; he would
therefore be the very last to scruple to use
secular words to express Christian ideas;
and as a matter of fact this is what we find
him doing in other cases also. He not only
employs philosophical terminology, but con-
forms to popular idiom.

But though it is true that he usually calls
his written sources by this general name of
Memoirs, yet in one passage (*Apol.* i. 66)
he calls them *Gospels* in such a way as to

indicate that he knew this to be their proper technical name. The passage is as follows:

" For the apostles, in the *Memoirs* which were written ·by them, *which are called Gospels*, thus handed down that they were commanded."

Is it not evident that in this passage Justin so far departs from his general practice of using popular words as to explain that not *Memoirs* but *Gospels* was the accurate title of his written records?

And in a similar incidental way he says in another place (*Dialogue,* chap. 103), that these records which he generally ascribes to apostles in a wide sense were compiled by " His (Christ's) apostles, and those who followed them "; thus giving prominence to the fact that some of the *Gospels* were written by *apostles*, and others by *the followers of apostles.*

Could there possibly be a more striking resemblance to the traditional authorship of our Gospels: two of which were written by apostles, Matthew and John; and two by

followers of apostles, Mark the follower of
Peter, and Luke the follower probably of
John ? [1]

We hold then that, without actually mentioning the *names* [2] of the writers of these
Gospels (which would have been entirely
out of conformity with his usual practice
when writing for outsiders), Justin has most
accurately described their authorship in a
way which can hardly be resisted by any
candid mind.

I must trouble you with one more passage
of Justin referring to his written source of
information before I go on to notice some of
the quotations themselves.

In the sixty-seventh chapter of the first
Apology he says :

---

[1] See a most suggestive paper by the Rev. H. R.
Poole, D.D., Senior Fellow T.C.D., on *The Origin of
the Gospel according to St. Luke.* (McGee, Dublin.)

[2] Justin, *Dialogue* 106, appears to quote St. Mark's
Gospel as "*The Memoirs of Peter.*" This is the exception to his usual practice ; and would point to the
fact, attested by early tradition, that Mark was the
interpreter of Peter, and drew his materials from him.

" And on the day which is called the day of the sun there is an assembling together of all who live in the cities or in the country, and the Memoirs of the apostles or the writings of the prophets are read."

Here then we have the written records of our Lord's life, which, as we have seen, contained what we now read in our Gospels, which were technically called Gospels, and were written by the apostles and their followers, placed on a distinct footing of equality with the prophets of the Old Testament, like Isaiah and Jeremiah, and read in precisely the same way that we now read our Gospels in the public service of the Church on Sundays.

From all this I think that we may fairly conclude that Justin knew and used our present Gospels ; and this presumption cannot be dispersed by a recital of the actual quotations themselves. For though we must admit great and frequent instances of inaccuracy in Justin's Gospel-citations, yet there are important considerations to account for this, as we shall presently see.

I shall now cite some examples of Justin's quotations,[1] that you may judge whether they be the very words of our Gospels or not.

Let us first take those which agree more or less with our St. Matthew.

Apol. i. 16.

But whosoever shall be angry shall be in danger of the fire. (*Matt.* v. 22.)

And whosoever compelleth thee to go a mile, follow with him two. (*Matt.* v. 41.)

And let your good works shine before men, that seeing, they may admire your Father in the heavens. (*Matt.* v. 16.)

Swear not at all, but let your yea be yea, and your nay, nay : whatsoever is more than these is of the evil. (*Matt.* v. 34, 37.)

Apol. i. 15.

Do not these things to be seen of men, otherwise ye have no reward of your Father who is in the heavens. (*Matt.* vi. 1.)

---

[1] A discussion and classification of these citations is given in Zahn, *Geschichte des Neutest. Kanons*, vol. ii.

Lay not up for yourselves treasure upon the earth, where moth and rust corrupt, and thieves break through ; but lay up for yourselves treasure in heaven, where neither moth nor rust corrupt. For where treasure is, there also is the mind of man. (*Matt.* vi. 19.)

Dial. 51.

The law and the prophets were until John the Baptist. From which time the kingdom of the heavens suffereth violence,[1] and the violent take it by force. And if ye will receive it, this is Elias, who was to come. He that hath ears to hear let him hear. (*Matt.* xi. 12.)

Dial. 49.

Elias shall come and restore all things. But I say to you that Elias has already come, and they recognised him not, but did to him whatsoever they wished. (*Matt.* xvii. 11, 12.)

Dial. 17.

Whited sepulchres, appearing beautiful

[1] Or (more probably) *advanceth violently.*

16

without, but within full of dead men's bones. (*Matt.* xxiii, 27.)

Dial. 112.

Who exalt themselves and desire to be called Rabbi, Rabbi. (*Matt.* xxiii. 7. 12)

Citations which appear to be from St. Luke.

Dial. 103.

His sweat fell down like drops, while He prayed and said, Let this cup pass away if possible. (*Luke* xxii. 44.)

Apol. i. 33. *Dial.* 100.

But the Virgin Mary, having received faith and grace, when the angel Gabriel announced to her, The Spirit of the Lord shall come upon thee, and the power of the Highest shall overshadow thee, wherefore also that which shall be born of thee is holy, the Son of God ; answered, Be it to me according to thy word. (*Luke* i. 35, 38.)

Dial. 76.

I give you power to tread upon serpents

and scorpions, and over all the power of the enemy. (*Luke* x. 19.)

Dial. 81.

Neither shall they marry, nor be given in marriage, but shall be equal to the angels, being the children of God, and of the resurrection. (*Luke* xx. 36.)

Dial. 105.

Father, into Thy hands I commend my spirit. (*Luke* xxiii. 46.)

Citations which appear to be from St. Mark.

Dial. 100.

And one of His disciples, who was formerly called Simon, he surnamed Peter. (*Mark* iii. 16)

Dial. 88.

Is not this the carpenter ? (*Mark* vi. 3.)

Apol. i. 45.

His disciples going forth preached everywhere. (*Mark* xvi. 20.)

Dial. 32.

He was taken up into heaven. (*Mark* xvi. 19.)

———

There are hardly any passages which look like formal citations from St. John;[1] indeed the special features of that Gospel rendered it unsuitable for quotation in controversy with those outside the Church; still Justin calls our Lord "the only-begotten" (*Dial.* 105) and "the Word" (*Apol.* ii. 6, and about twenty other places).

He also says (*Apol.* ii. 6), "by Him He created all things." He also refers to our Lord's words about the serpent in the wilderness (*Dial.* 94 = *John* iii. 14); our Lord curing persons who had been disabled from their birth (*Dial.* 69 = *John* ix. 1); the water of life (*Dial.* 14 = *John* iv. 10, etc.); the vine and the branches (*Dial.* 110 = *John* xv. 1); those who pierced the Christ (*Dial.* 64 and 118 = *John* xix. 34); the gathering together

———

[1] See however the remarks on Justin's use of St. John in Salmon's *Introduction*, p. 72, note.

of the scattered children (*Apol.* i. 53 = *John* xi. 52).

And one more extensive reference may be reserved for the end :

" Unless ye be born again, ye shall not enter into the kingdom of the heavens ; but that it is impossible for those who have once been born to enter into their mothers' wombs is evident to all " (*Apol.* i. 61 = *John* iii. 4).

Such then are the citations which Justin made from the written records which he had before him, which he called Gospels, and which, he said, were written by apostles of the Lord and the followers of apostles, and were read every Sunday in the Church service. The question is, whether these were the same Gospels which we now have or different ones.

We are logically bound to believe that they were the same Gospels, unless there be some insuperable objection to this view ; for otherwise we must postulate the existence and general Church use of a different set of

Gospels, which Justin used A.D. 150, but which had entirely disappeared and given place to our Gospels A.D. 172, when Tatian compiled his *Diatessaron.*

Now this is an extremely improbable hypothesis, and one which nothing but sheer necessity should drive us to adopt. Is there then this necessity?

Those who say, "Yes," support their view by pointing to the inexactness of Justin's citations, and say that they are so different from the kindred passages in our Gospels that we cannot believe that he used the latter. But this is a very inadequate reason for disturbing our conclusion; for, in the first place, Justin is noted for inexact quotations, of which we may find many instances where he refers to the books of the Old Testament, about which there can be no dispute. And, in the next place, Justin seems not to have reached a high standard of literary or artistic precision; for his arguments are often loose, and his language often wanting in finish. Besides, we cannot always be sure that Justin *means* to give a *verbatim* report of the words of one particular Gospel. On the contrary, we can point to some instances in which his object is clearly to. *combine* the words of the different Gospels, so as to present a full account of the particular matter of which he is writing. This is a most interesting point, for it shows that the germs of the *Diatessaron* of＊Tatian are to be traced in the works of his master and teacher Justin.

Let us cite some instances of this.

Apol. i. 33.

Behold, thou shalt conceive in thy womb (*Luke* i. 31), of the Holy Ghost (*Matt.* i. 20), and shalt bear a Son, and He shall be called the Son of the Highest (*Luke* i. 31, 32), and thou shalt call His name Jesus, for He shall save His people from their sins (*Matt.* i. 21).[1]

---

[1] Perhaps it is significant that Justin's words immediately following this composite quotation are ὡς οἱ ἀπομνημονεύσαντες πάντα τὰ περὶ τοῦ σωτῆρος ἡμῶν Ἰησοῦ Χριστοῦ ἐδίδαξαν. Was he conscious that he was using the words not of one but of two records?

Dial. 88.

I am not the Christ, but the voice of one crying (*John* i. 20, 23); for there shall come one mightier than I (*Luke* iii. 16) whose shoes I am not worthy to bear (*Matt.* iii. 11).

From these and similar instances[1] it would appear that Justin (like his pupil Tatian) did not hesitate to modify, by omission, addition, combination, or paraphrase, the words which he found in his Gospels. These had not yet been declared by the Church to have been divinely inspired, nor did Justin regard them in any other light than as authentic writings in which reliable history was recorded. There was no doctrinal reason to prevent him from handling them in this free way, and more especially when writing for unbelievers, and citing probably from memory. We may, therefore, conclude that the verbal inexactness of Justin's citations is no valid reason for doubting that the Gospels which he used were the very same which twenty-two years

[1] See additional note at the end of this chapter.

later formed the material for the *Diatessaron*, and which are the same Gospels which we now value.

But the remark which was made at the outset about Tatian must here be accommodated to Justin: that the Gospels cannot have been quite new when they were thus copiously used by him. They must have had an assured position in his time. They must have already won their way to recognition as the exclusively authentic form of apostolic tradition. And therefore we are justified in pushing them back at least twenty years before the first Apology of Justin, which was written about A.D. 150. This fixes A.D. 130 at the latest date at which they can possibly have been composed; and our next step must be to push them farther back into the very lifetime of St. John himself.

You will have taken note of the fact, that though Tatian and Justin make such copious use of our four Gospels, they never tell us the *names* of the persons by whom they were

written.[1] Our next witness will, however, in
the case of two of our four Gospels, give us
this information.

This witness is Papias, bishop of Hierapolis, a city which was only a few miles from
Colossæ and Laodicea, and which is mentioned in St. Paul's Epistle to the Colossians.

We must first say something of the *date*
of Papias, as this has been very variously
estimated by writers of opposite schools
of thought.

Some critics, like Alford, placed him as
early as A.D. 110; while others asserted that he
suffered martyrdom as late as A.D. 164. The
latter depended entirely on a passage in the
Chronicon Paschale, which was compiled in the
first half of the seventh century, and which
represented Papias as having suffered martyrdom at Pergamum about the same time when
Polycarp suffered at Smyrna. Bishop Lightfoot has however conclusively proved that
this passage of the *Chronicon Paschale,* which
is the only authority for saying that Papias

[1] See however p. 238, note 2.

suffered martyrdom, was a blundering transcript of a passage of Eusebius, in which,
after mentioning the martyrdom of Polycarp
at Smyrna, the learned historian went on to
give the names of three persons who were
martyred at Pergamum, Carpus and PAPYLUS
and a woman, Agathonice.

There are so many similarities between the
two passages that it cannot be doubted that
the one is a transcript of the other, and that
the scribe ignorantly substituted Papias, a
name with which he was doubtless familiar,
for Papylus, a name of unusual occurrence.
" If," says Lightfoot, " the last letters of the
word were blurred or blotted in his (*i.e.* the
chronicler's) copy of Eusebius, nothing would
be more natural than such a change."

Now we have *three* reasons for assigning
an early date to Papias.

The first of these is a statement made by
himself in a fragment which Eusebius has
preserved for us, that he was a personal
hearer of some of our Lord's own disciples:
we shall discuss the passage later on.

The second reason for assigning an early date to Papias is, that Eusebius says that he (Papias) gives in his writings an account of several miracles of which he had been told by the daughters of Philip, who lived with their father in Hierapolis, the town of which Papias was bishop; for whether this Philip be correctly described as the apostle, or as the evangelist, there can be no doubt that his daughters are the same persons who are mentioned in Acts xxi. 9 as prophetesses living at that time at Cæsarea.

Our third reason for assigning an early date to Papias is the distinct statement of Irenæus (who was to a certain extent his admirer) that he was a hearer of John, and a companion of Polycarp.

This Polycarp is supposed by some critics to have been none other than the Angel of the Church of Smyrna, whom St. John mentions in the second chapter of the Revelation.

At any rate there is no doubt that he was a disciple of St. John; and therefore, as

Papias was a *companion* of his, he too must have lived before the end of St. John's life, At least this is the most probable inference.

Influenced by these *three* considerations, Bishop Lightfoot and other safe critics assign A.D. 130 as the date at which Papias probably flourished and wrote his celebrated book.

And now as to that *book*. Where is it to be found? What was its character? And what is its bearing on our Gospels?

As to the first question, Where is the book to be found? You will probably be disappointed when I tell you that it is *lost*.

Though we are told by Church writers who saw the work and had it in their hands, that it consisted of *five books*, we have now only a very few extracts, which were fortunately transcribed by later writers, and have thus been preserved for us.

It is just as if the five books of Moses had perished, and only about twenty verses here and there had escaped, by being transcribed into the works of later writers.

Still the providence of God has left us

quite enough of Papias to enable us to come to a conclusion on the important point which we are discussing. We have first the title of the work; next we have an extract from the preface; we have then a few short extracts from the body of the work.[1] Let us deal with these in turn.

The title of the work was

ΛΟΓΙΩΝ ΚΥΡΙΑΚΩΝ ΕΞΗΓΗΣΕΙΣ,

"Expositions of Oracles relating to the Lord."

Now this title tells us two things: it tells us that Papias was an expositor, and it tells us what it was that he expounded. The five books of Papias, then, were *Expositions,* and he himself is classed by later writers among the *expositors* of the early Church, as Irenæus, Hippolytus, Clement of Alexandria, Pantæ-nus, and Ammonius. We have, therefore, got one step on our journey; for we have

---

[1] These extracts, which are quotations of Papias made by Eusebius and later writers, are to be found in the smaller Leipzig ed. of *The Apostolic Fathers.* See also for an English translation T. & T. Clark's "Ante-Nicene Christian Library," vol. i.

found that Papias had some record or writing before him, which he set himself to explain and expound, probably for the benefit of his flock in the diocese of Hierapolis.

What was this writing? It is called by Papias himself " Oracles of the Lord "; that is, Oracles relating to the Lord, or having the Lord for their subject.

With regard to the word " Oracles," we are familiar with several passages in the New Testament where it refers to the Old Testament Scriptures : but here the addition of the adjective *Κυριακῶν*, that is, relating to the *Κύριος* (our Lord Jesus Christ) transfers the word " Oracles " from their Old Testament sense to mean " the Scriptures which describe and have especially to do with the person of our Lord "; in a word, *the Gospels*. Accordingly, this word " Oracles " is found applied to the New Testament. Photius says that the Scriptures recognised by Ephraem, patriarch of Antioch, consisted of the Old Testament, and the Oracles of the Lord (*same Greek words*), and the Preachings of the

Apostles.[1] Here the expression " Oracles of the Lord " is evidently only another name for the Gospels ; and the same use of the word is found in Irenæus. Without entering farther into this question, we shall therefore take it as proved that the nature of the work of Papias was, a Commentary or Exposition of the written Gospels.

And if we omit for the moment all reference to the fragment of the Preface which Eusebius has preserved, and go on to the fragments of the work itself, we find Papias actually giving the *names* of two of the evangelists on whose work he is commenting.

The first fragment is as follows :

" And the elder said this also : Mark, having become the interpreter of Peter, wrote down accurately everything that he remembered, without, however, recording in order what was either said or done by Christ. For neither did he hear the Lord, nor did he follow him ; but afterwards, as I said, [attended] Peter, who adapted his instruc-

[1] See *Lightfoot*, pp. 172–176.

tions to the needs [of his hearers], but had no design of giving a connected account of the Lord's Oracles. So then Mark made no mistake, while he thus wrote down some things as he remembered them ; for he made it his one care not to omit anything that he heard, or to set down any false statement therein."

Now, all that need be said about this extract is, that Eusebius, the person in whose work it occurs, distinctly noted that it re- lated to Mark, *the writer of the Gospel;* and this was the universal opinion of Church writers.

With regard to Matthew, Eusebius wrote, the following statement is made (*i.e.* in the work of Papias) : " So then Matthew wrote the Oracles in the Hebrew language, and each one interpreted them as he could."

Here it is the opinion of Bishop Lightfoot that the past tense *interpreted* refers to a time long gone by when Papias wrote, a time when the first Gospel existed only in its original Hebrew form, and when there

17

was no recognised translation. This state
of affairs seems to have come to an end
before Papias wrote ; and Lightfoot thinks
that his words may be taken as implying
that in his day there was a recognised Greek
translation.

At any rate, whether that be true or not,
it cannot be denied that Papias in these extracts referred to Mark and Matthew as the
writers of Gospels. And we have the same
question to face again which we have faced
already, as to whether these were the *same*
Gospels which we now have. Well, no doubt
of this was entertained by Eusebius, or any
other Church writer. They all accepted what
seemed so plain and fair an inference ; and
which would have been accepted without
question in the case of any secular author—
that Papias was dealing with the Gospels of
St. Matthew and St. Mark as they were
known all through the history of the Church,
and as they are now known to us.

The sceptical hypothesis, however, is that
there was an original St. Matthew different

from, but the parent of, our St. Matthew, and
an original St. Mark different from, but the
parent of, our St. Mark ; and that it is these
originals, and not our degenerate transforma-
tions of them, on which Papias commented.
But there is not the smallest shred of evidence that there ever were Gospels of
Matthew and Mark different in scope and
contents from those which we now possess.[1]
Who does not see therefore that this modern
quibble has been adopted in despair by those
who dislike the miraculous character of our
Gospels, and would postulate anything,
however unlikely, for the purpose of dis-
crediting them ?

But perhaps some of you are mentally
asking the question, "Why does not Papias
tell us something of St. Luke and St. John?"
This is an improper question ; you should
rather ask, " Why does not Eusebius tell us
that Papias gives some account of St. Luke

---

[1] I say "different in scope and contents," because
it must be admitted that St. Matthew wrote originally
in Hebrew.

and St. John?" For Papias may have said ten thousand things in his books of Expositions which Eusebius did not think it necessary to quote, especially as he had a low opinion of his mental capabilities. Let me make my meaning clear by an illustration. Perhaps there is some one here taking notes of my lecture, who for some reason has neglected to record my remark about Justin's practice of combining the words of the different Gospels, or Bishop Lightfoot's clever discovery of the confusion of Papias with Papylus. Suppose that note-book were to come into the hands of a critic in five years' time, as the only available source from which information about my lecture could be drawn, would it be fair for him to argue that I said nothing about these two points, on the ground that there was no reference to them in the note-book?

In the same way it is very unfair to urge that Papias knew nothing and said nothing about Luke and John in his five books which are lost, on the slender ground that Eusebius has not seen fit to quote any such statements from them.

The general practice of Eusebius is, to record only *strange and unlooked for things* about those books of the New Testament of whose authority there was never any doubt in the Church; and so here he records of Mark that he was the hearer and chronicler of Peter's utterances, and of Matthew that he wrote originally in Hebrew.

Let us regret that Eusebius has given us no more of Papias, but let us not commit ourselves to the fallacy that because some of Papias is found in Eusebius therefore nothing which is absent from Eusebius can have been in Papias.

The points about Papias which we have now reached are, that he was an expositor of the Gospels, and that even the few extracts of his expositions which we now have refer by name to Matthew and Mark.

We must now glance for a few moments at the source and nature of his expositions; the former is plainly indicated in the extract from the Preface which Eusebius has preserved. I shall quote it according to the translation of Lightfoot :

"But I will not scruple also to give a place for you along with my interpretations to everything that I learnt carefully and remembered carefully in time past from the elders, guaranteeing their truth. For, unlike the many, I did not take pleasure in those who have so very much to say, but in those who teach the truth ; nor in those who relate foreign commandments, but in those [who record] such as were given from the Lord to the Faith, and are derived from the Truth itself. And again, on any occasion when a person came [in my way] who had been a follower of the elders, I would inquire about the discourses of the elders—what was said by Andrew, or by Peter, or by Philip, or by Thomas or James, or by John or Matthew, or any other of the Lord's disciples, and what Aristion and the elder John, the disciples of the Lord, say. For I did not think that I could get so much profit from the contents of books as from the utterances of a living and abiding voice."

According to this passage, you see that Papias lived in a place where and at a time when he could meet persons who, like Aristion and the elder John, had themselves seen and heard the Lord; or who had been companions of Andrew, Peter, Philip, Thomas, James, John, and Matthew. And you are informed that his general practice was to question such persons as to incidents about our Lord, and precepts which He gave. These apostolic traditions he treasured carefully in his mind, and when he afterwards wrote his expositions of the Gospels, he did not scruple to incorporate these incidents and sayings, and to give them a place with his interpretations.

Of the mere handful of these traditions collected and recorded by Papias, which have survived to our day, some seem foolish enough, and were probably picked up by the credulous bishop from some designing rogue, and not from hearers of the Lord.

Here are two of the foolish sort :

1. " As the elders relate, who saw John the disciple of the Lord, that they had heard from him how the Lord used to teach concerning those times, and to say, ' The days will come in which vines shall grow, each having ten thousand shoots, and on each shoot ten thousand branches, and on each branch again ten thousand twigs, and on each twig ten thousand clusters, and on each cluster ten thousand grapes, and each grape when pressed shall yield five - and - twenty measures of wine. And when any of the saints shall have taken hold of one of their clusters, another shall cry, " I am a better cluster ; take me, bless the Lord through me." Likewise also a grain of wheat shall produce ten thousand heads,' etc.

" These things Papias, who was a hearer of John and a companion of Polycarp, an ancient worthy, witnesseth in writing in the fourth of his books, for there are five books composed by him. And he added, saying, ' But these things are credible to them that believe.' And when Judas the traitor did not believe, and asked, 'How shall such growths be accomplished by the Lord ?' he relates that the Lord said, 'They shall see who shall come to these [times].'"

2. In this same fourth book of his expositions he relates the sufferings of Judas after he had betrayed our Lord. He says that Judas walked about in the world a terrible example of impiety, and then proceeds to give most minute and painful details of the torments which he endured, such as might be anticipated in the pages of a modern "penny dreadful," rather than in the commentary of an ancient and learned bishop.

You are not, however, to suppose that all the illustrations of Gospel narratives quoted by Papias are of this character; some are much more worthy of being seriously considered. Such are the miracles related to him by the daughters of Philip at Hierapolis, the resurrection of a dead man, and the drinking a cup of deadly poison without injury by Justus who was surnamed Barsabas, whom the holy apostles after the Ascension of our Lord put forward with Matthias as a candidate for the apostolate, and whom a little lower down Papias denominates by his proper name Joseph.

But it is time for us to draw to a close. I have not mentioned all the early vestiges of the fourfold Gospel, but have only endeavoured to supply a graduated scale by which those Gospels which at the beginning of our inquiry we found placed at the end of the second century and a hundred years from St. John may now be brought down step by step to the beginning of that century, and to the lifetime of St. John himself.

The first step down the ladder is from the days of Clement, Irenæus, and Tertullian at the end of the second century to Tatian, who composed his *Diatessaron* A.D. 172. The next step is from the *Diatessaron* to Justin Martyr, A.D. 150. The next step is from Justin to Papias, who commented on the Gospels about A.D. 130, and in whose commentary the Gospels themselves (so far as we know) were mentioned in words which implied that they themselves had been written long before.

There are many of our own friends and relatives who have a vivid recollection of the year in which O'Connell died and the famine occurred in Ireland, and who have printed in their memory the sayings and doings of that very eventful time. Now that requires a stretch of recollection reaching back forty-four years ; and if Papias may be credited with anything like as good a memory, why may not he in or about A.D. 130 have been able to recollect stories which were told him, and characteristics of his informants, so far back as A.D. 86 ? Why may not Papias, in short, have been personally acquainted with men who were youths at the time when our Lord Himself lived, died, rose, and ascended?

We are thus furnished with a chain of external testimony, which reaches back to the lifetime of some of the apostles themselves, which allows no space for the incubation of myth or the accretion of legend, and which, when properly grasped, cannot fail to bind us more firmly than ever to the personal and historical Lord Jesus Christ of the catholic creeds.

ADDITIONAL NOTE ON JUSTIN AND TATIAN.

BESIDES (1) *Apol.* i. 33 (mixture of Luke i. 31, 32, and Matt. i. 21), and (2) *Dial.* 88 (mixture of John i. 20, 23 ; Luke iii. 16 and Matt iii. 11), which are quoted on p. 247, the following composite citations should be considered :

(3) *Dial.* 51 (mixture of Luke xvi. 16 and Matt. xi. 12).

(4) *Apol.* i. 16 (mixture of Matt. iv. 10 ; Luke iv. 8 and Mark xii. 30).

(5) *Apol.* i. 19 (mixture of Matt. x. 28 and Luke xii. 5).

(6) *Apol.* i. 15 (mixture of Luke vi. 30 and Matt. v. 42).

(7) *Dial.* 15 (mixture of Matt. xxiii. 23 and Luke xi. 42).

Minute study of these and similar instances might lead to the conviction that Justin pursued the same practice of combining the words of the different Gospels which his pupil Tatian afterwards reduced to an art. In the first instance here quoted (see p. 247, note 1) he seems to be conscious that he is using a plurality of records. I cannot help thinking that if we had some examples of his public lectures to *Christians*, which would doubtless contain a larger proportion of citations from the Gospels than the three works which are extant, inasmuch as the latter were addressed to those who were not Christians, much light might be thrown upon the origin of the *Diatessaron* of Tatian. That work is so perfect in its way, that it is hard to believe that no previous efforts had been made in the same direction. It remains merely to point out four instances in which Justin and Tatian agree in a peculiar reading. In each of these cases the reading finds some support from other authorities also, which are given in Zahn.

(1) Justin, *Dial.* 88=Zahn's *Tatian*, p. 125.

"When Jesus went down to the water, a fire was kindled in the Jordan."

(2) Justin, *Ap.* i. 63 ; *Dial.* 100=Zahn's *Tatian*, p. 149.

" No one knows the Father but the Son, and no one knows the Son but the Father."

(3) Justin, *Dial.* 101=Zahn's *Tatian*, p. 174.

"None is good but one, My Father who is in the heavens."

(4) Justin, *Dial.* 17=Zahn's *Tatian*, p. 198.

"Woe to you, scribes, for you have the keys (plural)."

Butler & Tanner, The Selwood Printing Works, Frome, and London.